400c 80-4547

LANGUAGE FOR TEACHING

LANGUAGE FOR TEACHING

By

Hunter Diack, M.A.
UNIVERSITY OF NOTTINGHAM
INSTITUTE OF EDUCATION

PHILOSOPHICAL LIBRARY
NEW YORK

PUBLISHED 1967 BY
PHILOSOPHICAL LIBRARY, INC.,
15 EAST 40TH STREET, NEW YORK 16, N.Y.

*

ALL RIGHTS RESERVED

PRINTED IN GREAT BRITAIN
FOR PHILOSOPHICAL LIBRARY
BY COX & WYMAN LTD.

CONTENTS

INTRODUCTORY

OUR minds are seldom free from linguistic activity of one kind or another. When we are not using language on other people, other people are likely to be using it on us. Language comes to us in print by the acreage. It is hardly possible to buy any pre-packed commodity without buying print at the same time, and in these days of television we are constantly being subjected to a barrage of language in sound tied to pictures. Talkative people will deliver themselves of tens of thousands of words a day, and a man whose output is less than one thousand a day is likely to be regarded as a very quiet, if not taciturn, man. When we are not speaking or being spoken to, we are usually thinking and that is a process which is only intermittently dissociated from language if it is ever wholly dissociated from it at all. Even when we are day-dreaming we may now and then find ourselves fumbling for the right word to fill the gap in one of the sentences of our inner speech. Nor is linguistic activity confined to our waking hours. People have been known to talk in their sleep, sometimes with disastrous results. And one of Masefield's poems was copied down from an engraved tablet that he saw in a dream and remembered when he woke up. It has recently been claimed that one of the most effective methods of learning anything at all is what might be called the 'eiderdown' method—learning by gramophone record or tape while you sleep.

It seems clear then, that through any brain which is not comatose the traffic of words seldom comes to a halt.

To professional educators of all kinds language is of

very special concern. They not only use words profession-ally more than most people but they also have the re-sponsibility of training others to use both spoken and written language effectively. The teacher of young children has the problem of using words to communicate facts and ideas to children who are often without previous experi-ence of the things, the facts and ideas the words are con-nected with, or of the words themselves. Teachers also have to use words when teaching their pupils how to use words. At the later stages of education teachers are in-volved with language in more complicated ways, and more diverse ways: the language of the poet for example is different from that of the scientist, so different that specialists in the one discipline have been known to designate specialists in the other as 'illiterate'.

Inevitably, in the later years of school and during the undergraduate or training college years, a considerable amount of discussion goes on about language. Sometimes these discussions are planned and connected with one another in order to provide the student with a course of study. Often they arise incidentally out of the work in hand and therefore do not have the coherence of a planned course. Such a course of study is, however, difficult to fit into either the professional training year in a university department or the three years of the college course. There does not to my knowledge exist a book that contains between one pair of covers the kind of information that such a course might profitably contain. Even if the college syllabus is already too crowded to allow such a course to be established, a book setting forth language theory in the context of education is still likely to be useful both for the students' private reading and as a basis of discussion in general seminars. I have tried here to write such a book and it is one of my hopes that where this book is used it will promote that kind of thinking which leads to a weakening of the barriers that exist between the different subjects in this age of specialisation.

The basic unit of language is generally taken to be the 'word' and this is not normally regarded as one of the more difficult items in our everyday vocabulary. It is short, easy to pronounce and spell, and there is usually little doubt as to what it means. It appears quite normally in the speaking vocabulary of five-year-olds and when it does so they have, for them, a sufficient idea of what it means. Pupils, when they are asked to make particular words out of sets of jumbled letters, have no doubt about what they are expected to do, even though they may not in every case be able to do it. Nor do older pupils have any difficulty in understanding the teacher's intention when they are asked to write a précis in, say, 80 words of a 400-word passage. Yet put the question 'What is a word?' to a group of reasonably intelligent adults and very soon a lively argument will develop. In no time at all the group will find itself involved in a discussion of some of the unanswerable questions that are the stock-in-trade of philosophy.

Teachers in such a situation, for example, quickly find themselves wondering whether what they have been calling 'words' for years are really words at all. They have been in the habit of asking pupils to write down words and yet in the course of discussion come to the conclusion that no pupil ever wrote a 'word' but merely sets of signs that stood for words. Some members of the group may then shift their position and declare that essentially words are spoken and therefore *sounds* are intrinsic to words. It may then be pointed out that thought, with 'words', proceeds as often in silence as in sound. This gives the whole group further food for thought—both silent and vocal. Or again, these teachers remember that they have used arithmetic books in which appear such exercises as:

Write 6739 in words.

In the course of discussion, however, they come to realise that 6739 is as much a collection of 'words' as is 'six thousand, seven hundred and thirty-nine' since both are sets of signs for words, not words themselves. For years these teachers have been referring to signs like 5, 6 and 7 as 'numbers', but now find themselves questioning their own assumption, for if 5 is a particular 'number' how can the Roman 'V' be the same number? Are they not both signs for the number? And what is the connection between 5 and 'five'? The only way of reading 5 aloud is to say 'five'. Does this not imply that 5 is neither more nor less a word than 'five' is? If this is so, then the expression $3+2=5$ must be a sentence. At that point a lively discussion is likely to arise as to what a sentence really is. . . .

This book does not contain the answers to all the questions that are likely to arise in such discussions, but it does bring together some facts and ideas pertinent to many of the answerable questions. Furthermore, in chapter-appendages an attempt is made to show the relevance of the matters discussed to what happens in class- or lecture-rooms.

The general plan of the book is 'developmental', i.e. it traces the development of language in the individual from infancy through the school years to maturity, the later chapters fanning out to cover different aspects of language as used by adults in different disciplines. The developmental chapters are preceded by a general chapter about language and human communication.

Note
SIGN AND SYMBOL

In these introductory paragraphs I have used the term 'sign', with clarity, I think, in that context. The term has many meanings, however, and some writers have found it convenient to distinguish between 'sign' and 'symbol' leaving the latter term for words used *symbolically* as in 'The pen is mightier than the sword'. I have not made that distinction between the two terms. Ordinary usage works too much against it. I would point out, however, that 'symbol' is not in this book limited to what is visible. Speech, for example, consists of sound-symbols: the printed letter on the other hand is normally a visual symbol for vocal activity resulting in a certain sound; the printed word is a series of visual symbols standing for a series of sound-symbols that themselves stand for . . . well, the rest of this book is largely a completion of that sentence.

Chapter 1

SOME GENERAL CONSIDERATIONS

WHAT makes the discussion of language difficult is the fact that abstruse philosophical questions are never very far from the threshold of consciousness when the nature of language is being discussed. The reason for this is clear, even though it sometimes seems that very little else is. These questions settle on the fringe of this topic because it is impossible to get very far in a discussion of language without considering the relationship between words and things and as soon as that happens we are likely to become involved with questions about the nature of our awareness of things.

A simple example will illustrate this point. Let us suppose that I find myself at a tea-table with a young and eager student of chemistry whose knowledge is freshly effervescing in his brain. Before us there is a bowl of ordinary white granulated sugar. I am scarcely aware of it, only sufficiently so to put a teaspoonful of it in my tea knowing that it will dissolve and have a sweetening effect. When the young chemistry student looks at it, however, different things may take place in his mind even though his outward actions are the same as mine. He may be momentarily conscious of the process of crystallisation, of the chemical formula for that particular kind of sugar, of the place that that kind of sugar occupies among the large number of substances classified as 'sugars' by the chemists. I am not suggesting that the young chemist will *necessarily* think on these lines but that he *may* do whereas it is impossible for me, in the present state of my knowledge, to have in my mind, for example, the chemical formula for ordinary household sugar. There is then the 'thing' called sugar; it may be thought of in two different ways by two different people—and one may assume in a number of different ways by other people. Can it be said, then, that the sugar is *perceived* differently by various persons? If so, is that difference in perception brought about by the fact that different people have acquired different sets of words, the chemist, for example, having his way of thinking about sugar differently orientated because he knows the chemical formula and what lies behind it? Is there then the implication here that our perception of the external world is influenced by the language we have acquired? Furthermore, if the word 'sugar' means one thing to me and another thing to the chemist, where is the 'real meaning' to be found? Or is the idea of a 'real meaning' not perhaps a fantasy? But perhaps the 'true meaning' is the sugar itself. Yet how can we know the sugar itself if different people have different ideas when they think about this substance? But perhaps in thinking about the sugar itself we ought to forget such concepts as are implied in the chemical formula and be guided solely by our sense-perception of it. And yet is it not true that the sugar itself is *not* our sense-perception of it? Perhaps, then, the name 'sugar' is not the name of the thing itself but of the complex of sense-perceptions through which we are aware of the substance. Does this then mean that it is a delusion to think that we are ever speaking about the things of the external world but always about the shadows of reality that are in our minds? It is a small step from the position on which that question is poised to the position maintained by Berkeley that there is no reason to believe in the existence of anything outside the mind—and that is an issue around which the thunder of philosophical argument has for centuries rolled.

The simplest view of language sees it as a system of signs standing for things or relationships between things. These signs are in the first place auditory (speech) and in the second place visual (writing and print). Speech comes first because writing is a development of speech and, of course, print is a development of writing. In this simple view the 'signs' may be, and often are, likened to labels, and the idea of words as labels is a useful concept for the teacher to have, especially at the primary stage. This is well recognised by teachers. In infant schools throughout the country you will find the written language presented to children as a system of labels. Various objects in the rooms are labelled—*table*, *chair*, *window*, and so on—and the recognition of these printed words in the context of the appropriate real things is normally part of the child's introduction to the skill of reading. At this stage the label idea of words is, of course, implicit; there is no attempt to teach the children that words can be regarded as a kind of label. One would not expect children of that early age to be able to think about the nature of words as distinct from the meaning of words. And yet by pointing out the 'label' nature of words at an early age a teacher may be doing useful work. It has frequently been maintained that the tendency of the human mind to confuse the 'word' and the 'thing' is one of the main sources of intellectual error. The implanting, therefore, at an early age of the idea that words are merely labels loosely attached to the things they signify may weaken this tendency in later years even though at the time of the implanting the child has no conscious idea of the full significance of what is being learnt.

Labels, however, are used in different ways. The various labels in a library are a direct guide to the whereabouts of particular books. In most libraries sections are prominently labelled, e.g. Travel, History, Biography. Furthermore, each book is labelled by means of its title and the name of the author as well as by a code of letters and numbers. Since many of the books are not in the library at any one time, there is a further series of labels which are kept in a prearranged order—the card-index. The labelling in the classroom is of a very different order; it is altogether a more random affair. There is no logical connection between the window and the chair nor between the names for them; the only reason why the names for these things are put in front of the pupils at the same time is that both these things are present in the classroom. Now language as a system of labels is more like the labelling in the classroom than like the index-labelling of the library. It is a peculiarity of languages in general that none of the natural languages is *planned* as a unitary whole. There is no necessary logical connection between the form of one word-label and that of another even though both refer to things within the same category. By 'form' I mean here the sounds of the words and, by logical extension, their appearance in print or writing. For example, although 'horse' and 'pony' both refer to things that are to a very great extent similar, there is no similarity whatsoever between the two words whether spoken, written or printed. By no stretch of the imagination could anyone who knew and understood the word 'horse' deduce that a smaller edition of the same animal would be called a 'pony'. Nor on the other hand could anyone who knew and understood the word 'horse' deduce from that information the meaning of the word 'pony'. One result of this diversity is that most of the words in a language have to be learned as separate units. Another is that, as a system of signs, language is untidy; it is not cut and trimmed and designed for efficiency.

There is for some people an attraction in the idea of having a planned language. Probably more people are thinking of such a thing at the present time than ever before because, with almost instantaneous communication throughout the world, the need for an international language appears to become more and more pressing. A planned language would have to be a tidier language than any of the natural languages and one of the first things the planners would have to think of would be how to avoid the anomaly of having very different forms of label for the same kind of thing. In such a language, for example, there would be a certain similarity between the words *boil*, *stew*, *fry* and *bake*. It might be thought that a unit such as *cul* (from *culinary*) could be taken to mean *cook*. If then *q* (from *aqua*) were taken to mean *water*, then *culq* would mean *boil* (cook in water). Let us further give *ad* (from *adipose*) the meaning *fat*, then *culad* could hardly mean other than *fry* . . . and so a streamlined language might be built up. But in no time at all changes would creep in. Someone would use the term *culq* to mean *boiling* in connection with the washing of clothes, and that has nothing to do with *cul* whatsoever.

There we have one strong argument against an attempt to fashion a tidy artificial language; it would not remain tidy if it were put into general use. A stronger argument, however, rests on the emotional roots of natural languages. No natural language is merely a tool of the intellect. Each has deep emotional roots in every person whose mother tongue it is. The planned language has no such emotional roots. It is probably this emotional aridity that accounts for the failure of all artificial language so far devised to gain acceptance of the kind their inventors hoped for.

Untidy though it is compared with the library index or the artificial language, our ordinary language is nevertheless the means whereby our experiences are classified and recorded. On an earlier page I posed, rhetorically, the question as to whether our perception of external things is modified or determined by the language we have. It is not difficult to show that this is indeed so, provided we remember that language is more than the sound or the printed letter, it is the repository of previous experience.

Suppose there is put before you a sheet of paper on which are placed: a small irregularly-shaped brown object rather like a crumb of cork, a small shred of what looks like thin brown paper, some black specks and a rough-surfaced brown object about the size of your finger-nail. What is similar about all these objects? To the naked eye very little. Can you now from the description find that they are all in one way essentially the same? The description is not full enough? You have as much information from that verbal description as a child of two actually looking at them but for whom they have not yet been classified by means of a common name. But now I give you the word 'seeds'—and even in your mind you 'see' them differently.

There we have a greatly foreshortened view of what is constantly happening to a child when he is learning his mother tongue. He is for ever being told that things that are different are the same—not in so many words but implicitly by the use of common nouns—animal, furniture, flower. A process of classification is continually going on. Through learning the simple common words of everyday speech the child gradually and unconsciously acquires knowledge that in many instances took the human race ages to arrive at. In acquiring that knowledge the child imposes a certain order and relatedness upon his sense-perceptions.

The simple use of words as labels occurs frequently and effectively in everyday life.

You go to a railway booking-office, say, and ask for a second-class return ticket to Brighton. The booking-clerk runs his hand along the pigeon-holes and produces the right ticket.

A teacher says to her class, 'Take out your reading books.' The books are unlikely to be arranged in the child's desk as the tickets are in the booking-office, yet the children all select the right one.

Here we have the essence of effective linguistic communication at the simple label-level. It may be illustrated by a diagram so simple that every primary school child can, and should, draw it.

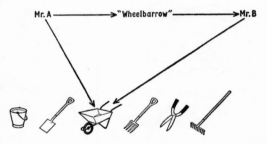

The word enables Mr A. to get Mr B. to think about the same thing that he is thinking about.

That diagram, though grossly over-simplified, is, I think, a basic diagram in teaching. It has the great merit of showing with the least possible complication what we are usually trying to bring about when we are using words between one another: we are trying to get the other person to think about the same thing as we are. When the two lines converge closely, the communication has been effective. We are usually also trying to get the other person to think of that thing in the same way as we are, but that is something this simple diagram does not show. Nor at the early stages of education should this complication arise in an overt form.

The vital omission from that diagram, the one which causes the gross over-simplification, is that it gives no indication that experience of the thing intervenes between the two minds concerned and the thing itself, and so, for anything but the very simplest treatment of the process of linguistic communication, this basic diagram must be elaborated slightly to a form something like this:

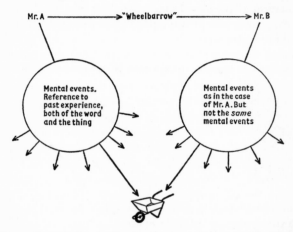

Here the circles indicate the mental acts of reference and of association. The arrows projecting from the circles indicate the fact that the associations are not all concentrated in the direction appropriate to narrowly efficient communication. In simple matters like the transaction at the railway booking-office or the pupils taking out their reading-books, there would probably be no associations standing in the way of efficient communication. Even the child who is reluctant to take out his reading-book because he is backward at reading understands what is required of him. He does not 'see' the reading-book as his teacher would like him to, but he has no doubt about what she is referring to. Matters are by no means always as simple as that, however; the lines of reference do not always converge.

In referring in passing to the philosophical questions that stand poised on the edge of any discussion of language, I mentioned the venerable idea that it might be a delusion to think that we are ever speaking about things but always about our particular experience of things. This seems to me an inescapable truth. It also leads to a curious paradox. At those times when linguistic communication is efficient, it does not matter that we are not speaking about the things themselves, because it is a condition of efficient communication that the *experiences* of the persons concerned should be sufficiently similar. I have no doubt of the similarity of the experiences to mine when I see someone touching a stove that is too hot for comfort; I therefore am confident that I understand what he means when he tells me about it. Similarly I have regular proof when I go into a tobacconist's that his experience of the appearance of tobacco tins is sufficiently like mine. Therefore the very efficiency of linguistic communication for so much of the time in ordinary things makes me tend to think that individual experience has a smaller role to play than philosophically I know it must have. I have to make a mental effort to remain conscious of the fact that the 'thing itself' stands somewhat apart from the language that refers to it.

One fact that stands in the way of clear and efficient communication is that the 'things' referred to are often very complicated. The more general a term is the more 'things' are included in its reference. Because, for example, the term 'music' includes so many varieties of that art, two persons who agree with one another that they are fond of music might disagree very strongly when it came to actually listening to music, having only then discovered that it was different kinds of music they were thinking about.

The communication diagram would then assume a form something like this:

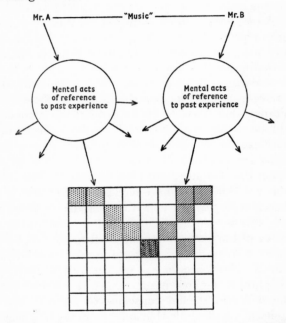

The 'thing' referred to in this case is not represented by a simple square but by a grid. Each square in the grid represents a sub-class in the wide range of musical forms. The stippled squares represent those that Mr A has in mind; the hatched, those that Mr B. has in mind. There may, or may not, be overlap in the sub-classes of the 'thing' referred to; there can never be complete overlap in the experiences referred to. The rectangle itself represents the whole set of things referable to under the name 'music'.

The inclusiveness of general terms often allows people to think they are speaking about the same thing whereas in fact they have different things in mind.

Another main cause of inefficient communication is connected with the extent to which an individual's experience of the 'thing' referred to is special to him, together with the degree of insight he has into the processes underlying the language he uses.

Let us suppose that a man has seen someone very dear to him knocked down and killed at a pedestrian crossing. An experience of such intensity is likely to be to some extent relived not only when he is near that particular crossing but also whenever he sees the conventional signs indicating a pedestrian crossing no matter how far that crossing is from the one where the accident occurred. The beacons and zebra markings are immediate signs of the crossing. But the name 'pedestrian crossing' is also a sign of that particular kind of thing. If the name does not recall the 'thing', then the name might as well be a blank label since it cannot be said to have any meaning. Since, if it is really functioning as a name, the term 'pedestrian crossing' will recall the 'thing' for the man we are speaking about, it will also tend to recall the tragedy and the emotional upheaval connected with it. Here the emotional force may be so strong that, even though his language may suggest that he is speaking about pedestrian crossings in general, his mind may be almost entirely concerned with the intense personal experience he had in connection with one particular pedestrian crossing. In such a case the communication diagram would follow this form:

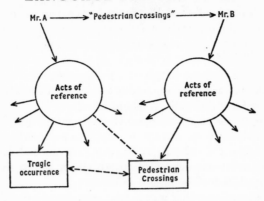

Here the dotted line indicates a minimal reference to pedestrian crossings in general on the part of Mr A. This diagram conveys an idea of the situation as it might be conceived by an outsider not himself involved in the situation—us, for example, taking an objective view of what is happening. Neither Mr A. nor Mr B. need be aware that their conversation has departed so markedly from the conditions necessary for effective communication. The conversation, we may suppose, is about the effectiveness of pedestrian crossings as a means of reducing the danger to pedestrians. In such a discussion, if Mr A, has allowed his emotional experience to overrule his judgement, he will almost certainly speak less about pedestrian crossings in general than about one particular crossing and what happened there—even though the form of his expression suggests that he is speaking about pedestrian crossings in general. If Mr B. on the other hand is the sort of man who in such arguments is guided by relevant statistics, he will find it extremely difficult to get Mr A. to accept anything he says.

The definition of language as 'the index of experience'

emphasises, among other things, this kind of divagation. Words may indeed be compared to labels, but these labels acquire their significance through their association with our experiences of the 'things' they signify. Your words have no significance for me unless I am able to relate them to some 'thing' and I can only do that if somehow or other I have had experience—it may be second-hand—of that 'thing' in association with the word. In order that I should be able to think of the same 'thing' as you are when you use the word, I must have learned to associate with your words experiences not too different from those you have associated with the words. So, when you address words to me, I am able to refer to my past experiences, and the experiences I select in the process of reference are sufficiently similar to yours. In most ordinary situations they are so very similar that it does not occur to either of us that they may be different—and yet there are occasions when the similarity is more illusory than real, and the cause of the illusion is the very efficiency of language in the great majority of ordinary situations.

It is possible that the analogy of 'index' may be creating an impression of language as a somewhat static kind of docketing system. And yet, however fixed and static an index looks, when it is functioning it is making information accessible to the mind which may then do something with it. When it is creatively active, the mind takes the information and with it effects new combinations. So the index: language analogy is not a wholly superficial one. Constructive and creative thinking is a matter of using language, with its references to past experience, in such a way as to arrive at new combinations. Is there any man-made product that did not 'exist' as a mental concept before it existed in material form? In the formation of that mental concept linguistic operations were intrinsic.

The operation of using words to discuss words bears a certain resemblance to trying to lift oneself by one's own bootstraps. The difficulty of the operation is apparent in the paragraph I have just written; it stems from the fact that when we use the words 'language' and 'word' we may be effecting a separation of the word from the 'thing' (or 'experience of the thing'). That they should be regarded as separate we have seen to be desirable, but if the separation is too complete then we cease to be discussing language or words and may as well be discussing 'pum', 'frim', 'prot' or any other nonsense syllable; what may seem to be a word is not one unless it has meaning; that meaning depends upon a reference to experience. It does not, of course, follow that if we do not understand something we have heard or read, that something is not language; it may read or sound like gibberish to us but may be the essence of clarity itself to someone else who has had the appropriate experience.

The defining of the term 'experience' is not easy. Ostensibly it means anything whatsoever that has happened to a person. It may even mean experiences of which he was unconscious at the time and of which he has remained unconscious since. After all, in Freudian psychology, unconscious experiences are regarded as the more significant ones. The wider the application of a term, however, the more thinly spread does its meaning become. So the phrase 'reference to past experience' does not give a very clear idea of what I have in mind in this discussion of word and meaning. If, however, the word 'analogous' is inserted before 'experience', then a certain clarification takes place.

The experiences that give a word meaning are of the following kinds:

1. They are analogous to the original experiences

through which the word acquired any meaning for us at all.

or

2. They are analogous to an experience that is analogous to the original experiences.

or

3. They are analogous to an experience that is analogous to an experience . . . in a series of mental events that only death will finally bring to an end.

or

4. Each 'experience' is a set of mental events which includes the word as well as the thing. Therefore the analogy may be between, say, the sound-pattern of the word and the sound-pattern of another word leading to another 'thing' that in itself is not analogous to the first 'thing'.

or

5. They may not be analogous at all but be merely associated in time.

An example will clarify further.

I look at the tree outside my window. On this day of wind and sun its sound is like the sea (analogical reference to Wordsworth's sonnet to Milton) and the branches are heaving and tossing in the wind. Unwinding the tensions of logic, I let my mind go free and, in seconds, quicker than I can put more than a fraction of them down, a series of references passes through my mind: a particular tree 400 miles from here: a church and Immanuel Kant: a starling's nest: the Adirondacks: Dorothy Wordsworth: Keats: Guernica: a line from a Hungarian folk-song: roast goose: the Dead Sea: Attila of the Huns. . . . The words I have put down are merely slight indicators of what is in each case a complicated manifold of recalled experience. To give a full account of what lies behind those indicating words would not be possible in a much longer book than this one. But I can briefly give an intelligible account of one, of how the roast goose got into the tree.

Very often when I hear the sound of wind in trees, I think of tall poplars against the vast skies of the Hungarian *puszta* which I visited in my student days, a semi-desert which, when the wind tossed the poplars, was filled with the sound of the sea; there then come into my mind words from a Hungarian folk-song which, translated, mean *The wind is blowing and the rain is raining*: I heard that song on my first evening in Hungary after a dinner of roast goose!

So there we are: this tree—the Hungarian poplars—(direct analogy): wind in the trees—wind in the song (direct analogy): song—roast goose (time-association).

James Joyce's *Ulysses* and *Finnegan's Wake* are extensive explorations of mental events and their structure in this aspect. Mathematically trained readers might find here also a hint of the structures of space-time geometry.

Past experience is for ever exerting its pressures upon present experience—the mystery always is; which part of past experience and why? There are, of course, established patterns for different people within which variations of the analogies will take place. The artist looking at the tree may characteristically be thinking of its shape and the distribution of light and shade, but some present occurrence, e.g. the sight of a small boy on a dangerously slender branch, may greatly change his reactions. On the other hand the timber merchant in looking at the tree may, through long-established mental habit, instantly begin estimating what footage of usable timber could be got out of it. And yet in the normal occasions of life we assume that others, looking at the same object as we are looking at see what we ourselves see. And similarly with language: we assume that when we speak others will refer in their minds to the same things (or experiences of things) we are referring to by our words; and when we hear someone else speaking, we assume that his references are the same as ours would be if we had spoken the words. If these assumptions were not in part justified, then communication by means of language could not take place. On the other hand if the assumptions were always fully justified, then communication between individuals or groups would not present the serious problems it so often does and misunderstandings would not be among the main characteristics of human life.

In this chapter I have given a bare outline of a theory of language trimmed to the necessities of teaching. It is a simple view but not, I hope, naïve. I have regarded language as a tool and, for the immediate purposes, have assumed those using it to be doing so as a means of straight communication, that is, having something they want to say without any prevarication to someone who is willing to listen. It has been asserted that language was given to man so that he could conceal his thoughts. With that aspect of it I have not here been concerned. Nor have I, except in a passing reference, said anything about the deliberate use of language to persuade, mislead, or deceive. Our first concern should be, I think, to consider language as an instrument of straight communication.

THE PRACTICAL ASPECT

It is my intention to provide at the end of each chapter a few practical notes showing what application the ideas expressed in the body of the chapter may have in teaching. This chapter has paid a fair amount of attention to the conditions which interfere with the effectiveness of communication. The idea that words may not mean what they seem to mean, however, has little relevance to the primary stage of schooling. There is no point, and indeed there may be harm, in showing children that communication may be more difficult than it seems. It does not, however, follow that the 'sign' theory of language outlined here has no relevance to teaching at the primary stage. On the contrary it is at this very stage that the foundations are best laid for fuller insight into language later on.

For very young children, games and puzzles that have to do with our awareness of things and that employ language in connection with our awareness of things are useful not only because of the linguistic and perceptual exercise they give to the children but also because of their potential diagnostic character from the teacher's point of view.

One such game is a variation of the well-known Kim's game. The variation takes the form that the children are given the names of the objects they are going to see. Normally Kim's game consists of the uncovering of, say, a dozen different articles placed on a table or tray. The children study the articles silently for a minute or so and are then, after the articles have been hidden from view again, required to name as many of them as they can remember. The suggestion I make is that the game is played normally once and then the teacher tells them it is to be played again but that this time, before they see the articles, they are going to be told what the articles are. They are, of course, different articles the second time. It will usually be found that the children are more successful in the second form of the game. The scientifically-minded reader may ask here about 'practice effect' and if it worries him greatly he can take the usual precautions of giving a few practice trials to begin with. With older classes in the primary school it will not come amiss to ask the pupils why in their opinion they are better at recalling the objects after they have been given the names of them. The answer it is reasonable to expect from the brighter child is that when you are told the name of what you are going to see it is just like seeing it, so that when the cover is taken off the object it is like seeing them a second time. A more adult answer, which, however, does not conflict with the answer I have given, is that when you know what you are going to see you take less time to recognise it and so have more time for memorisation.

Here are some questions which have a bearing on the subject of awareness and which children find interesting. They are asked to name things in the following categories:

1. Something that you can see and hear.
2. Something that you can see but not hear.
3. Something that you can hear but not see.
4. Something that you can feel but not see.
5. Something that you can smell but not see.
6. Something that you can see, smell, feel, and taste, but not hear.

Specimen answers to these are 1, a cow; 2, the moon; 3, thunder; 4, the wind; 5, gas (of the domestic kind); 6, cheese. In some of the higher primary classes there may be bright boys who will disagree about some of the answers. Occasionally, for example, an awkward little customer will argue that lightning is part of the thunder so that you can see something of the thunder. It is all to the good that there should be some argument; it shows active interest.

This little game can also profitably be played in reverse, that is, the things are named and the pupils asked to name the senses by which we become aware of these things.

Arising out of this activity can come a vocabulary-enriching activity in which the teacher collects from the whole class orally all the words they can think of connected with each of the senses and here a great amount of work can be done. If we take, for example, the sense of sight, we might have from a group of children the following words: look, dim, hazy, watch, see, clear. But then we go on to what it is that we see about something and we get a further classification, of size, colour, shape. We may go on from there to words relating to size, words relating to colour, and words relating to shape. Here, however, I would emphasise that without the experience the words are meaningless. Many of the words given will be so familiar to even the youngest children that the experience can be assumed, but the activity must not be allowed to become a verbal activity only. If, for example, in connection with shape a child gives the word 'oval', which cannot be assumed to be in every child's vocabulary, then that shape should be drawn on the blackboard, either by the pupil who gave the word or by the teacher. It might be thought by some teachers to be a useful lead towards precision of language to point out the difference between the perfect oval and the egg shape—also perhaps between the rectangle which is often called 'square' and the geometric square.

I would make another point here, namely, that the exploration of vocabulary in this way results in a classification of words according to similarity or relatedness of idea —the model is of the Roget *Thesaurus* type, not the alphabetically arranged dictionary. The keeping and compiling of their own dictionaries by the children is very useful, but I believe that a combination of dictionary and 'thesaurus' is more valuable. This would be too big an undertaking for each child, but with children taking it in turns to be 'editor' under the close supervision of the teacher a most useful compilation would grow rapidly. It would have to be in loose-leaf form. Let us say that on page 1 are collected all the words dealing with shape and on page 19 all the words dealing with weather (because the 'thesaurus' brings within its covers words arising out of many different discussions), then in an index at the end, alphabetically arranged, the word 'shape' will appear with a reference to page 1 and 'weather' with a reference to page 19. If any set of words runs over to another page, e.g. the 'weather' group, then that page may be numbered 19.1 or 19a. The advantage of vocabularies arranged in a systematic totality like this is that since they substitute logic and association for the purely conventional alphabetic order, the words in this arrangement are more easily recalled.

These simple suggestions will no doubt fit on to, if not indeed coincide, with, what some teachers do already, but I hope that they will stimulate further developments along the same lines. At the same time I would emphasise that *experience* is the necessary accompaniment of all language activity, for without the sensory experience of the things the words refer to, the words have no meaning.

I have given most space in this section to teaching at the early stages because the relevance to those stages of what is said in the body of this chapter does not exactly spring out of the pages.

About the later stages there is at this point less to be said. If what I have said in the chapter has any relevance to secondary teaching at all—and I believe it has a great deal—the diagrams I have given put the position clearly.

The first simple diagram should, I think, be introduced at a convenient time during the last two years of primary education. It is perhaps not until the second or third year of secondary education that the significance of the later diagrams will begin to be appreciated. There is hardly a passage that the pupils are likely to read, however, to which these diagrams are irrelevant.

Chapter 2

EARLY SPEECH

IT is not very much more than a century since the beginnings of speech in a human being were first studied with scientific care. The human being whose early linguistic activities were thus observed was the first-born son of Charles Darwin and the observer, not unexpectedly, was that child's father. The account of these observations was not published until nearly forty years later, but even so, although other studies of the same phenomena had meanwhile appeared, that account must still be placed among the early studies of the development of speech in children. Since those days a great many studies have been published and in recent years devices for recording and analysing sounds have become increasingly available, with the result that on the library shelves and in the periodical rooms of the academic libraries there is such a mass of detailed information in this field that, for sheer lack of time and opportunity, most teachers must remain ignorant of most of it. This, however, is a different kind of ignorance from that which was characteristic of even the most advanced thinkers in education not so very long ago.

When, in *Emile*, Rousseau set out his views about the early speech of children, he produced a series of statements in which the results of shrewd observation sit in uneasy companionship with what reads like echoes of old wives' tales. At one moment we find him shrewdly pointing out that children may not hear words spoken to them as distinctly as the adult does; at the next we find him, with his romantic ideal of the simple life, declaring that the children of peasants always speak clearly because they have to speak loudly and clearly to make themselves heard in the open fields. We find him pointing out with considerable acumen that even when a child gives the correct form of words in answer to a question, it cannot be assumed that he has understood the question, for it may be that the adult has merely read the right answer into the child's words. On the other hand he advocates keeping a child's vocabulary small and argues that one of the reasons why peasants are generally shrewder than townsfolk is that their vocabulary is smaller. Of the processes by which the child came to speak his first words Rousseau had nothing to say except that he assumed imitation and thought that in the earliest years the vocal organs were stiff and only gradually lent themselves to the reproduction of the sounds heard. Even this slight treatment of early speech is far ahead of most earlier writers on education who merely assumed a mastery of the mother tongue. The first sentence of Roger Ascham's *Scolemaster*, for example, is: 'After the child has learned the eight parts of speech, he must be taught the joining of substantives with adjectives.' A fair-sized library could now be filled with books that might be taken as a vast preface to Ascham's opening sentence—and yet the idea behind that sentence has very nearly disappeared from the literature of education altogether.

Anatole France described language as 'the sounds of the forest corrupted and complicated by arrogant anthropoid apes'. He was thinking of the origins of language itself and that is a topic with which, according to the American linguist, Sapir, linguists have ceased to concern themselves seriously, because the evidence is hidden in the mists of pre-history. That the earliest cries of children are not essentially different from animal cries is, however, very widely accepted. Asking the question, Why does a baby cry?, Darwin in his book *The Expression of the Emotions in Man and the Animals* suggested that the answer might be the same as the answer to the question, Why does a lamb bleat? 'He pointed out,' says Lewis (*How Children Learn to Speak*), 'that the natural cries of living creatures are expressive in this sense: that the bleat of a hungry lamb is just as much a part of the activity of his body as all the other movements that he makes in the urgency of his need for food . . . The cry of the hungry baby is expressive in this same sense. We see the contortions of his body, the kicking and the struggling; we hear the cry produced by the excitement of his vocal organs. The cry expresses to us that the baby is hungry. If we take heed of it, this is the beginning of language for him. Out of his expressive cries the whole of a child's speech is fashioned.' A few paragraphs further on, Lewis points out that when Darwin said that a child's cry could be called expressive of his discomfort he did not mean that the child deliberately sets out to express himself, but that the sounds he makes—and indeed all the bodily movements at the time—are *to the mother* expressive of the child's state. If we put this in language that fits into the theory of language as outlined in Chapter One, we would say that the child's first cries are signs 'which we interpret' rather than as 'being expressive', for the term 'express' and its derivatives so often in normal usage carry the implication of intention (e.g. How should I express it?). It would be almost as accurate to say that a rain-cloud by its dark heaviness expresses a desire to precipitate in rain as to say that a child is *expressing* discomfort at so early an age, for there too in predicting rain we are treating phenomena as signs. It may be thought, however, that this is carrying logic so far as to insult the dignity of the human baby who after all, unlike the cloud, does have feelings and desires and does gradually learn to express them.

The view that the child's first cries are of a simple animal nature might lead us to expect that all over the world these first cries are the same, and this appears to be so. The Eskimo baby wrapped in his sealskins makes the same noises as the Kikuyu baby basking in the tropical sun. And yet the surprising thing is that long before there is any sign of what can be called language, indeed *within a few weeks of birth*, the baby's characteristic sounds begin to vary from the archetypal pattern. The Eskimo infant is now making sounds that do not appear in the Kikuyu repertoire at that age. These changes are generally taken as an indication that already at so early an age the infant is responding to the sound-patterns in his environment. The Eskimo mother is soothing her child in a different language from that used by the Kikuyu mother and the changes that occur show already a rudimentary form of 'imitation'. I put the word 'imitation' within inverted commas here for two reasons: first, there is not necessarily any resemblance between the sounds that now appear newly in the child's repertoire and the sounds of the mother's voice, second, here, as with the term 'express' there is no question of a conscious attempt to imitate by the child.

Lewis's classification of the early sounds of babyhood into 'discomfort' and 'comfort' cries has been widely accepted. The discomfort sounds are the earliest of all. In the first days of life, silence usually means that all is well in the baby's world. There is no mistaking these discomfort sounds; they are urgent, strident, not easily ignored. The 'comfort' sounds have a different character. With normal children they appear about the fifth or sixth week. When the child has been fed and is to all appearance satisfied with the turn things have taken in his young life, he begins to make sounds that we may reasonably describe as being of a goo-goo variety.

The infant-in-arms is not, however, merely making sounds; he is also hearing sounds—both the sounds he himself makes and the sounds that reach him from the external world. And yet 'hear' is one of those ordinary little words that are deceptively simple. It is, as a moment's reflection shows, possible to be within hearing of a sound and yet not hear it; it is possible for the ear-drums to vibrate and yet produce no effect, no conscious effect, in the brain. This is indeed not only possible, but necessary, a necessary accompaniment of the ability to select and to pay attention. The only way in which we can be sure that a child is hearing anything is by the observation of his behaviour, and the curious, observed fact about babies is that even at the end of the first week they will respond to the crying of other babies by crying themselves, though they will not respond to other sounds that are just as loud. After a few weeks the sound the baby responds to most definitely is the sound of his mother's voice. Most other sounds will produce no response. He will ignore passing cars, the whirr of a lawn-mower, the cooing of pigeons, the barking of dogs, but let his mother speak within hearing range and he is instantly on the alert. This is a sound which he has learned to invest with meaning—very much perhaps as Pavlov's dogs invested the ringing of a bell with meaning— meaning in the sense that one 'thing' has become a sign for something else. In a highly generalised way the sound of his mother's voice has become the sign of comfort— food and warmth. The forming of the association has, of course, been helped by the fact that, softly and gently though his mother may speak, she is often close to him while she does so. She even sometimes whispers in his ear and we know from our own experience that such whispers are often clothed with thunder,

Some observers maintain that several months before the most optimistic mother would claim that her child has spoken his first word it is possible to detect different 'meanings' (the 'meaning' being in the observer's mind) in the sounds he utters, meanings less general than mere discomfort and comfort; it has been maintained that one kind of discomfort cry is associated with hunger and another with a desire to be picked up and caressed. There is no general agreement about this, though the possibility of differentiation between types of cry so early does not seem so very remote. What is generally agreed, however, is that soon after he has begun to make comfort sounds in addition to the discomfort ones the child enters what is usually called the 'babbling' period. This is a period during which making sounds for the fun of it seems to be one of the infant's main preoccupations. The infant may be said to be playing with his voice and in the course of this play he learns something about how different sounds are made. Here again we must rid ourselves of any idea of conscious intention. This is learning of the most completely natural kind—through play. The infant babbles as naturally as the puppy chews or the kitten pounces.

All students of the development of speech agree that this babbling or 'pre-verbal vocalisation' is extremely important in laying the foundations for learning to speak.

A word that has come much into use in learning theory in recent years is 'feed-back'. A simple example of the principle of feed-back in operation is the thermostat controlling the temperature of a room. The initial control comes from a human being who sets the pointer on a dial. Thereafter the heating apparatus is controlled, or moderated, by its own activity. The temperature of the room becomes a source of 'information' to the heating apparatus. When the temperature rises beyond the set point, the apparatus switches off; when it falls below, it switches on. That is to say, the results of its own activity are fed-back into the system.

In a *very* much more complicated way this principle is operating during the child's babbling stage—and indeed ever after. The sounds the child makes are heard by him both through the ear and by bone conduction. Experiments at Harvard indicate that in this process of 'auditory feed-back', as it is called, bone-conduction and hearing by ear are significant in almost equal proportions. As is so often the case, light is thrown upon normal development by what happens in abnormal cases. In their long study of deaf children, the Ewings of Manchester came to regard the babbling period as of extreme importance. In severely deaf children there may be, according to these authorities, absence, or almost complete absence of babbling. Such children do not have the capacity to any measurable degree for hearing themselves through bone-conduction. The amplification of their own voices through hearing aids is 'in all these cases the basis on which the ear-to-voice link or auditory feed-back is developed'. The Ewings also testify that the nearest-to-normal 'phonation' that they have heard from severely deaf children has resulted from accustoming them to rely on hearing their own voices in infancy and early childhood, i.e. through some form of amplification system. A reasonable deduction from these facts is that this auditory feed-back is not only a means whereby the child comes to know which sounds he is making but is also a stimulus to further voice-play.

It should be noted that this same principle of feed-back is of importance in so far as the kinaesthetic sense is concerned, the sense of knowing what our muscles are doing.

The child not only moves his lips and tongue but is 'told-back' through the neural circuits what has happened.

On the basis, then, of all this voice-play, the child moves towards the stage when at some time which cannot be clearly defined he speaks his first word.

Progress towards the meaningful use of words proceeds through such infinite gradations that with any particular child, however carefully observed, it is impossible to say that on such and such a day at such and such a time he spoke a word rather than merely made a sound. Any opinion about the matter with reference to any particular child will greatly depend upon the previous experience of that child by the observer, and that closest of observers, the child's mother, is likely to place the time rather earlier than others will do, not only because of a natural, though possibly unconscious, desire to shine in the child's reflected brightness but also because her experience has given her special information about that child's incipient language. If someone from outside the family hears the child say *'goga'*, he may very well fail to single that duosyllable out from the many other sounds that the child is making. The child's mother, however, may from previous experience know that that is the sound the child has made in response to her saying 'Chocolate'. If the child does say 'goga' and the evidence is that in saying so he means chocolate, is he then speaking? That is a matter of argument. Perhaps the best compromise is to say that the child is speaking but has not yet got round to speaking English.

The power to imitate sounds is obviously quite basic in learning to speak, but the word 'imitation' must in this context be given a somewhat different meaning from that which it normally has, because of the gradualness with which the child acquires the ability to produce sounds that are instantly recognisable reproductions of sounds heard. The making of any sound at all in response to a sound heard has, I think, to be regarded as the first step in imitating; it is *something* that in response to a sound the child makes another sound instead of merely, let us say, waggling his toes.

Detailed case-studies of children learning to speak are perhaps of little more than academic interest to teachers in schools for the normal child. Certain general principles that can be derived from these studies have, however, a very direct bearing upon what goes on during the early school years. It is with these general principles that I am now concerned.

1. The child's first cries have a purely emotional basis. Even his babbling must be regarded as expressive of a state of feeling, and certainly when the child first begins to use what are unmistakably words he uses them largely to serve his emotional needs. Even when a child has reached fluency in speech and is capable of speaking about the things he sees, such as raindrops on the window-pane, much of his chatter, though it appears to be concerned with external things, is merely a way of calling attention to himself—an expression of his desire for care and attention. This is often the case with his innumerable questions, his Why this? and Why that? Often the natural curiosity which is there at the beginning of series of questions spills over into a demand for attention. So when a child appears to be speaking about something outside himself, he is often in fact merely seeking love and attention.

This is frequently the case in school. Indeed, is it not often the case with adults?

2. It can be confidently asserted that the child does not hear words as the adult does. Children have to learn to hear. I do not mean by this that they have to learn to distinguish between sound and silence but that distinguish-

ing between sounds is a matter of learning. Distinguishing between sounds is also a matter of classification: this sound is the same as that sound and different from this. When the child is learning to speak and has reached the stage of beginning to be able to reproduce words with approximate accuracy, it will be noticed that he characteristically reproduces only part of the word. A child, for example, says 'pane' for 'aeroplane'. Why? Is it because in a longish word like that the last syllable has swamped the earlier syllables and in his effort to remember the whole word he has forgotten the beginning of it? Is it because in his pre-verbal vocalisation or in his first spoken words the sounds represented by 'pane' have occurred more frequently and have therefore become easier to reproduce? Here we are reduced to sheer speculation because the sounds the child reproduces cannot be taken as an accurate indication of what he has heard. What does seem clear is that inevitably a form of auditory analysis of the words heard is taking place, *must* be taking place. This, I think, has some significance for the learning and teaching of reading where it can be shown that the visual analysis of the printed word is taking place long after the aural analysis of those same words has ceased to be in the same sense necessary.

3. At the age of two and a half months or so the human baby is normally very responsive to the sounds of voices. Any sound said to him will get another sound in response. If the mother says Boo, the child will respond with a sound that need not have any rememblance to the sound he has just heard – da, mama, goo-goo; any sound will do. Several observers, however, have noticed that two or three months later the child is not nearly so responsive in that particular way. Darwin at first thought that his son had begun to imitate words at the age of four months, but it was not until the child was ten months old that his

father was certain that the child had actually begun to imitate the sounds heard. Darwin's interpretation of 'imitate', however, was the normal rather narrow one in which recognisable success in imitation is implied. What was happening during the six months that elapsed between the time Darwin thought imitation had begun and the time he was sure it had? We have here a phenomenon which has been noted by a number of observers, an apparent regression rather than further development. The period of free and spontaneous vocal response to sounds heard is followed by a period during which the child does not respond to sounds with sounds. During this period the mother may begin to think that the infant is not progressing as well as she had assumed it reasonable to expect.

Since the phenomenon has been widely observed and seems to be typical, it is reasonable to look for explanations that will show this curious phenomenon to be a part of the process of *development* in the normal child. The first explanation that suggests itself is that, as the child's experience of heard sounds increases, so his ability to discriminate between sounds increases and it seems possible therefore that he is discouraged from responding to one sound with *any* sound through his awareness—his twilight awareness—of the fact that the sounds he makes are not the same as the sound he is replying to.

This theory possibly appears at first sight far-fetched. In putting it forward, however, I have in my mind the observed fact of the pleasure very young children take in 'finding the thing that fits'. It is one of the common-places of child psychology today that security is a basic need of young children. The basis of security is that things should turn out as we expect them to do from past experience, i.e. that the accidental should not obtrude too often or too drastically. For this to be possible, experience in all its variety must be set in a tidy framework. Things have to be seen, heard, felt, tasted and so on as the *same* or as *different*—the two basic concepts of sensory and intellectual life. It does not seem to me, therefore, a rash step to postulate as a built-in tendency this urge to find the thing that fits. Is this not what creative artists of all kinds are in their maturity for ever seeking? More obviously is it not what is continually being sought in mathematics and the sciences? We must accept it as a universally observed fact that normal children by the end of their first year are not only able to imitate words with great accuracy but take delight in doing so, is it therefore, all these matters being taken into account, very far-fetched to suggest that there is a period during which the child rejects the sounds which do not match the sounds heard and would rather remain silent than respond with a sound he has begun to learn 'does not fit'?

Lewis deals with this problem from a different point of view and gives a shrewder explanation. Yet the two explanations do not seem to me exclusive. He writes:

Our problem, in fact, is to explain how it is that these earlier responses lapse, and this seems inexplicable, so long as we take imitation as an isolated activity. But if . . . we continue to observe his vocal responses to speech in relation to his general development, we certainly do not find that these responses merely cease; what happens is that they are mostly replaced by behaviour of a different kind. The child, in fact, begins to respond to the meaning of what he hears; there is a corresponding inhibition of simple vocal responses to heard speech.

The important point here is that *meaningful* response, which may take the form of doing something rather than merely making a sound, is beginning to over-ride what may be called the 'automatic' response to sound stimulation.

The principle that emerges from these considerations is

that, supremely important though linguistic development is, that development even at the earliest stages is not a matter of speech alone but of speech linked with activity of another kind. The overt speech is not rightly thought of in isolation but as part of the total response to a situation: so much so that even the absence of spoken sounds may be a sign that a development towards fuller language ability is taking place.

THE PRACTICAL ASPECT

What bearing have these facts about the earliest speech of children on the class-room thinking and activity of the teacher? Since nearly all children have acquired a basic vocabulary before they reach school age, it could be argued that the exceptional cases ought to be the concern of remedial teachers and that, therefore, the teacher of normal children need not be greatly concerned about the child's previous linguistic development—or lack of it. This is to take far too narrow a view.

Although the phrase 'we are teaching children, not subjects' has been put to some curious uses, it nevertheless stems from an important educational truth, namely, that whatever happens at whatever time in school is part of the child's *living* as well as learning. The school is continuing a process that began with the child's first day alive; it is only a figure of speech to say that the child is starting a new life with his entry into school. To maintain that the child's pre-school years are of little concern to the teacher is as much as to say that the teacher is a mere instructor. But the infant teacher, especially, is not an instructor; her concern is 'the cure (i.e. care) of souls' more than the training in skills. Training in skills there certainly must be, but that is ancillary to the cure of souls. Failure to learn to read, for example, is an important failure only because of the effects it has on the child's development and it is the child's whole development that must be the teacher's care, so far as it is within her power. A necessary sequel is that some knowledge of the early speech development of children is part of a teacher's basic equipment—and not the infant teacher's only.

One or two specific points may be made in addition to this general statement:

Language, we have seen, has an emotional origin. The teacher who has fully accepted that fact will not readily lend herself to the view that language is no more than a mere tool whose technical use has to be mastered. There is indeed little danger of this happening in infant schools, but too often in junior schools the pressure of selection examinations has resulted in a mechanical treatment of language.

What a child is when he arrives in school depends to a great extent on what happened to him during the pre-school years when he was gradually drawing towards proficiency in speech. Sometimes those experiences are of a kind that noticeably affects his proficiency in language in school. For example, Lewis has pointed out two simple causes of backwardness in speech. The first is over-attention on the part of a parent or parents. The child who has his every need attended to almost before it arises will not learn the practical value of speech nearly as quickly as the child of parents who are less attentive. The latter, feeling a need, utters a cry and with parents only normally attentive that cry is responded to with reasonable frequency and reasonable promptness; so he learns that his cries have an effect. The second of Lewis's instances is the obverse of the first—the case of the neglectful parent. The child who cries or calls and habitually gets no response does *not* learn that his voice is effective; in his circumstances, it is not.

Chapter 3

THE ACQUISITION OF MEANING

CHAPTER 2 dealt largely with the process of learning to make sounds; but sounds without meaning are not language. *Meaning*, which was referred to only in passing in that chapter, is the main concern of this chapter which deals with some aspects of the acquisition of meanings by the child.

The gradations of progress towards effective imitation in speech are, as we have seen, fine enough to be described, non-mathematically, as infinite, yet it is doubtful if they outnumber the gradations in progress from the twilight meanings of infant speech to the fullness of meaning we expect (but do not always find) in the speech of adults.

One aspect of the problem of meaning was implied in the reference in Chapter 2 to the young chemist and the bowl of sugar, namely that though both the young chemist and I could use the word 'sugar' as a label for the same substance, yet because of his training in chemistry his meaning for the word was very much fuller than mine. This points to one of the universal truths about language — the existence of different levels of meaning. Further, since I could learn, say, the chemical formula for that type of sugar, it can also be said that the acquisition of meaning is a process that goes on for as long as any particular brain is alive. This is not in the same way true of the acquisition of the sheer physical skill of speech. Quite early in life, say by about eight years of age, the developing human being has had enough practice in listening to

spoken words and in speaking himself to be able to pronounce all but the most tongue-twisting words in the
language if he is given the opportunity of hearing them
first. He can repeat not only single words but fairly complicated sentences. There will indeed be an improvement
in the fluency and the effectiveness with which he speaks
his mother tongue, but for the vast majority of people the
improvement will not be very great. The great majority of
conversations carried on from day to day do not call for
greater skill in speech *as a skill* than is possessed by the
average 8-year-old. The acquisition of meanings is a very
different matter. It is a continuous process. The brain that
is not acquiring new meanings is moribund. I do not mean
only the acquisition of new words with their meanings, but
also the acquisition of additional or fuller meanings for
words already familiar, that acquisition of meaning which
brings about the difference between the brain surgeon's
concept of 'brain' and that of the millions of people to
whom the word signifies little more than 'grey matter
inside the head associated with thinking'. So between
adults there are indefinite gradations in the levels of
meaning. The gradations we are mainly concerned with in
this chapter, however, are those that lie between the
child's first overt responses to spoken sounds and his
acquisition of the ability to communicate thoughts and
feelings by means of spoken sounds that are unquestion-
ably those of his mother tongue.

Does the presence of a gooseberry leaf *mean* food to a
caterpillar? Does the sight and smell of an impala *mean*
food to a lion? Did the sound of a bell come to *mean* food
to Pavlov's dogs? Does the sight of his keeper at a particular time come to *mean* food to a chimpanzee? Does the
sight of his bottle come to *mean* food to a baby? Does a red
signal light mean 'Stop' to an engine-driver? Do the letters

D

in a word *mean* the sounds in the spoken word? It is possible to express in prose everything that a poet *means* by a poem?

The word 'mean', as we see in these questions, may be, and indeed is, used to cover a great variety of mental events. These questions are roughly graded. There is a universe of difference between the concept denoted by 'mean' in the sentence about the caterpillar and that denoted by the same term in the sentence about the poet. So great indeed is the difference between these two usages that the first usage might well be taken to be figurative only. The gradations on the scale, however, may be so fine that it is doubtful whether in fact one ought to postulate any difference, for example, between the sentence about the chimpanzee and his keeper and the baby and his bottle in so far as 'mean' is concerned. The situations are almost interchangeable, for many a young chimpanzee has learned to associate his bottle with food and many a baby has learned to associate his keeper, or nurse, with food.

We saw in the introductory paragraphs of this chapter that in the ordinary processes of communication words are used and interpreted at different levels of meaning. These questions demonstrate that we may use the word 'mean' itself in a way that implies 'levels of meaning' of a different kind. No one would argue that 'mean' in the sentence about the caterpillar and the gooseberry leaf has the same connotation as that same term in the sentence about the poet and his poem. The analogy between the two situations is extremely thin and yet if the two situations were not analogous in their shadowy fashion 'mean' would have no meaning at all in the first of the sentences. This points to one of the difficulties embedded in the whole discussion of language—the difficulty of preventing the analogies implied in words from being so far extended that terms cease to have definition, as has very nearly happened to the word 'mean' in these sentences.

The analogies between human and sub-human behaviour are particularly insidious, chiefly because so many of them are inescapable. Since the questions about the chimpanzee and the baby are interchangeable, can we deny that the human baby is learning to associate a sign with an object in the same way as the chimpanzee is? Both being without language, it is doubtful if we can. Therefore it can be argued that the kind of meaning the baby has acquired at that stage is of the same quality as the chimpanzee's. It is not difficult, however, to reject the word 'mean' in the sentence about the caterpillar and we may feel that all 'in-built' behaviour falls into a category in which the word 'mean' is not apt. But then we think about the behaviour of, say, ants and bees, and begin to wonder. Few people watching the buzzing and scampering activity fail to see a comparison between factories or cities. The inhabitants of the colonies seem to *know* what they are doing, which is as much as to say their activities have *meaning*. Questions arise. How does the ant *know* that the larvae of the greenfly can be kept and 'milked' as cows are by human beings? How does the bee *know* to make all its honey-cells six-sided? And here the word 'know' is performing the same dis-service as the word 'mean, did in the series of questions. Realising this, we may decide that the word 'know' like the word 'mean' must be kept out of discussions of 'in-built' behaviour. Ants and bees, we decide, do not *know*; they merely *do*. But then we read that by means of a curious 'dance'—an elaborate form of communication by means of gesture—one worker bee can communicate to another information about the whereabouts of nectar-supplying flowers, and we wonder whether information can be transmitted without *knowledge* and whether after all the word 'know' may not be legitimately used of some forms of in-built behaviour. And yet the question is not so puzzling if we postulate that *knowing* of a characteristically human kind is that form of knowing in which awareness of self is immanent. The human being is, or may be, capable not only of knowing but of being aware that it is he who knows, or even that it is he who does not know, and this is a kind of knowledge which does not seem to be accessible to any other creature on this planet. As a corollary to this, it is necessary to accept that no in-built or un-learned behaviour, however complicated, implies this kind of awareness.

While this distinction between awareness and non-awareness may be regarded as a definitive one in stating the difference between human and sub-human learning, it cannot be regarded as the only important one. Of decisive importance, too, is the fact that human beings can in a sense turn there into here, can bring the past into the present and can to some extent mould the future by bringing to bear upon it the experiences of both past and present. This they are able to do because of the fact that the meanings embodied in words are their past experiences, and not only their own first-hand experiences but those of the human community in general. Even the most intelligent animals, the apes, have no ability comparable to this. Apes have been reported to have a sound-language and while there are recorded instances of apes producing special sounds like *Nga! Nga!* on seeing their food, which might no doubt be translated as *Aha! Bananas!* there is no recorded instance of an ape producing his special 'word' for bananas when the bananas are not visible. Some time before the young human being is able to imitate words successfully, he is able to do what the fully grown ape cannot do—use sounds to indicate something that is not physically present to his senses. Lewis, for example, records that at 18 months his child, whose attempt to say 'chocolate' was 'goga', crawled to a drawer where the chocolate was normally kept and said 'goga'. This behaviour indicates the beginning of release from the tyranny of immediate perceptions. This tyranny has been noted many times by Piaget and at varying stages of development. The babe-in-arms for example, who has displayed interest in an object and has handled it, who has seen that object covered up before its very eyes, will immediately behave as though the object had ceased to exist. With children as old as four years, Piaget has shown many times that how a thing *looks* will over-ride the child's logic: for example, the child is shown two balls of plasticine equal in size; before his eyes one is rolled out to a sausage shape and the child will declare that it is now bigger. Piaget's experiments and conclusions have certain weaknesses, but there can be little doubt about the validity of his argument that the immediate perception exerts a tyranny over the child's thought.

The release from this tyranny clearly does not come suddenly nor all at once and it appears in different forms continuing, as in optical illusions, into adult life. And yet as early as 18 months we note the beginning of release from one form of it and it comes through language. The term Piaget uses throughout his work on child development as a key term in his theory is 'conservation' which might be translated as the 'holding-power of the mind', the power in the example given of holding on to the idea of the equality of the plasticine balls in spite of the change of shape. Suzanne K. Langer, who in her *Philosophy in a New Key* (O.U.P.) has some penetrating things to say about language maintains that the 'concept-holding' power of language is the essential core.

The fact is [she writes], that our primary world of reality *is* a verbal one. Without words our imagination cannot retain distinct objects and their relations, but out of sight is out of mind. Perhaps that is why Köhler's apes could use a stick to reach a banana outside the cage so long as the banana and the stick could be seen in one glance but not if they had to turn their eyes away from the banana to see the stick. Apparently they could not *look* at the one and *think* of the other. A child who had as much practical initiative as the apes, turning away from the coveted object, yet still murmuring 'banana' would have seen the stick in its instrumental capacity at once.

She goes on:

'The transformation of experiences into concepts not the elaboration of signals . . . is the motive of language. Speech is through and through symbolic and only sometimes signific.'

The word 'concept' presents some difficulty even though the processes of concept-formation have been much studied in recent years. A difficulty is that there is no definition of the terms which would allow one to say that when a child has acted in such a way he has now reached the conceptual stage of development, for concept-formation, like the acquisition of meaning, is a continuing process. What one can legitimately say is that the child who by his behaviour shows that he can think of something when it is not immediately evident to his senses has reached the stage of thinking conceptually—at the most primitive level of concept, perhaps, but nevertheless conceptually. A child who names a thing and uses the name of the thing effectively is thinking conceptually.

If we examine the events that must *necessarily* have taken place before a child can use a simple word like 'cup' meaningfully, the basis of the statement which concludes the previous paragraph may become clear. It is not suggested that 'cup' is the child's first word, merely that it is among his earliest words. Here then is the minimum list of events that must have taken place:

1. The child will have gone through an extensive period of voice-play during which, through the interaction of his sense of hearing and his kineasthetic sense, he will have learned a great deal about the use of his voice-muscles, to the extent of being able to produce particular sounds at will and in a specified order.

2. It is unlikely that he will have seen only one cup. On the contrary there will have been transmitted to the visual centre of his brain messages which have been stimulated by the reflected light from many cups seen from many angles. Sometimes a cup will be seen without a handle because the handle is hidden from vision. Sometimes it will be seen with a straight line across the top, sometimes with an elliptical top, sometimes with a circular top. Sometimes it will be seen at a distance when, if his only information were the pattern of light on the retinae of his eyes, it would be seen as smaller than his thumb-nail. At other times it will be so close as to fill most of the visible world. These things will happen whether he has seen one cup or many cups. This vast number of varying visual impressions have, however, all, in one bundle we may say, been associated with that other vast series of mental events which results in the utterance of the simple word 'cup'. From a great variety of visual impressions there has been abstracted the concept with which the name 'cup' is associated.

3. The events so far mentioned are not disconnected, however, from events in other areas of the brain. Hearing, kinaesthetic, visual, touch (for he will have handled the

cup smell (for he will have drunk milk or fruit juice from the cup) taste (for the same reasons)— all the areas of the brain associated with these senses will have been recording sensations connected with the thing called 'cup' and, in addition to these, at least the areas concerned with the movement and the recording of the movement of the voice-muscles.

4. The cup will not have been experienced in complete separation from other things in his visible, audible, smell-able, tasteable and tangible world, nor from the inner world of his own sensations. It will have been experienced in company with sensations of discomfort through hunger or thirst, sensations of comfort with the appeasement of hunger or thirst; he will have experienced it along with comforting or nagging sounds from his mother. And so his emotional life is involved in this storm of cerebration about a tea-cup.

5. He has acquired the ability in saying the word 'cup' to recreate in his mind parts of those constellations of experience and at the same time to abstract from those constellations the permanent concept of 'cup', recalling chiefly the appearance of it, yet not the appearance as seen, say, in a photograph but an abstract into which are fused many of the varying shapes the cup has taken when seen from many different angles and from many differing distances.

These events are of incredible complexity, but they are not attended by *difficulty*. The *potentiality* of speech in its initial complexity is inherent in all normal human beings. What is necessary to turn potentiality into achievement is a linguistic environment. When the environment is favourable and the child has crossed the threshold of language, his progress is quite astounding.

Once a child has grasped the idea that things have

names, he becomes avidly interested in discovering these names. This avid interest is one of the most noticeable things in the early speech development of children. 'What is that?' is the characteristic question at one stage of his development, and he means, 'What is that called?' He is given the answer, 'That is a tractor' or 'That is a dandelion' as the case may be and neither parent or child is worried by the fact that the name is not the thing, that 'tractor' is not a tractor and 'dandelion' is not a dandelion. 'A rose is a rose is a rose,' wrote Gertrude Stein—and was she thinking that the name is not the thing and no amount of repetition will make it so?

In the comments on the events necessarily preceding the meaningful use of a name it was suggested that the ability to speak about a thing, in the sense of naming it, in its absence implied conceptual thinking. That is to say, the names are not rightly regarded as mere labels attached to the objects even though, as suggested in Chapter 2 the 'label' idea of language is useful in explaining to children how words work. The child who is so busy adding to his list of names, however, is not merely collecting verbal labels; he is at the same time exploring the world of concepts.

For a considerable time [writes Suzanne Langer], playing with conception seems to be the main interest and aim in speaking. To name things is a thrilling experience, a tremendous satisfaction. Helen Keller bears witness to the sense of power it bestows. Word and conception become fused in that early period when they both grow up together.

Pleasure in playing with conceptions ... thrilling experience ... tremendous satisfaction ...

That is not over-written or exaggerated. Anyone who has been at the receiving end of the child's questions at this stage of his development, anyone who has overheard the child speaking to himself, who has listened to his tales of the doings of imaginary companions, who has been allowed to share the child's private language (such names as 'gobbledonk' for larder and 'cronky' applied to all things that will not stand up to what he regards as reasonable wear and tear)—any such person will not only have witnessed the child's excitement and pleasure but will have shared it as well, and may even have come to the conclusion that the separation of intellectual from emotional response is highly artificial at this stage of development at least.

Ogden in his *A B C of Psychology* (Routledge) states that soon after the child has mastered the 'word' he enters upon the most talkative stage of his development and may speak as many as 20,000 words of running talk in one day. How many different words are there in this output? And how many concepts? To discover the number of different words is much easier than to discover the number of different concepts. All that is necessary in order to discover the number of different words is to record the words and then count them. This task has been made easier by the invention of recording machines, but though theoretically very simple, it is still, as an earlier commentator expressed it, 'fraught with methodological difficulties'. The children will not always speak when the investigator is present; recording equipment, when hidden, fails to record many words and, when visible, may inhibit speech. A child will understand many words that he does not himself use and therefore information obtained from a sampling test based on the comprehension of words will not be an accurate reflection of the child's operational speaking vocabulary. Seashore's researches into this problem brought the astonishing result that the American first-grader has on the average a vocabulary of 23,700 words (only 8,000 of them being attributable to grammatical changes of form). The first-grade child is 6–7 years of age. On the other hand A. F. Watts found that the average 5-year-old in London had a vocabulary of 2,000 words. M. E. Smith in 1926 published a study of vocabulary in much younger children and obtained, among other figures, the following: at 2 years of age an average of 272 words in a group of twenty-five; at 3 an average of 896 words in a group of twenty; at 4 an average of 1,540 words in a group of twenty-six; at 5 an average of 2,072 words in a group of twenty. The average I.Q.s in the groups of 3-, 4-, and 5-year-olds were 109, 109 and 108 respectively. No. I.Q. was given for the 2-year-olds. Burroughs published in 1957 the results of a study of the speaking vocabulary of school children of ages 5–6½ in the Midlands of England. There were 165 boys and 165 girls in the sample. Students in training colleges recorded the words spoken by the children over ten ten-minute periods during which every device was used to get the child to talk. The number of different words collected in this way was 3,504, an average of 273 words per child, with 56 words in the shortest list and 578 in the longest. In this investigation there was clearly no attempt to discover the total vocabulary of the children but rather to record the words most likely to be used by children in talk during their first years in school.

The present writer, while engaged in the study of language and perception, was able to record the number of different words spoken in one day by a child one month short of 3 years of age. They numbered 221. It is not easy to categorise grammatically the words in a child's vocabulary because at the early stages the single name of an object will imply a whole sentence. Nevertheless these words were used in running speech and in meaningful contexts and had therefore grammatical quality although it was impossible to record the grammatical aspect at the same time as the recording of the words was being carried on. From the list itself, however, the following rough grammatical classification can be drawn up:

Nouns : bacon, ball, banana, basket, bell, biscuit, blackboard, bonfire, book, box, bread, breakfast, bus, butter, button, cardigan, chair, chin, Christmas, cigarette, clothes, coal, coat, cocoa, cup, daddy, dinner, dog, doll, face, fire, floor, frock, girl, goose, hand, hat, jam, juice, kettle, kitchen, letter, man, marmalade, matches, microphone, milk, mincer, moment, mummy, noddle-box, paper, pencil, penny, piece, piggies, place, plate, pussy, roof, room, rose-bush, sandwich, scissors, shoe, skin, spoon, steps, sugar, table, tea, telephone, things, toe, tummy, weather-cock, window, word, vacuum-cleaner, we-wee.

Verbs : are, aren't, bend, bring, brought, bump, can, clap, clean, come, could, cut, dance, did, do, don't, draw, drink, drop, feel, fell, find, get, give, go, harden, have, help, is, lie, light, like, look, lose, made, am making, manage, might, need, open, pick, please, reach, read, say, saw, see, shall, should, stood, smell, take, taste, thank, told, touch, try, turn, want, was, wash, watch, wonder, would, write.

Adjectives : big, both, busy, clean, clever, empty, first, grilled, late, little, mine, naughty, nice, open, ready, right, rough, some, sweet, warm, and the articles: a, an, the.

Pronouns : I, he, him, it, me, we, you.

Conjunctive words : and, though, where, what.

That the names of things should so greatly predominate at this stage is not surprising, but the considerable number of verbs in the list indicates that this child was well past the stage of being content with one-word sentences (i.e. the name of a thing alone being used to express a variety of statements about the thing, or indeed about the child itself as, for example, 'Car!' meaning *There is a car!* or *I want a ride in a car!*) There are very few conjunctive words and yet the fact that they are present at all indicates that already the child has acquired a certain dawning knowledge of the sentence-structure. One must be careful here, however, not to read too much into the word 'knowledge' as used in this context. Just as the child has no knowledge of the complexities involved in giving a thing a name, so he has no knowledge, in the full sense of the term, of why words go together as they do. The synthesis of words into sentences certainly occurs early in children's speech, but only because it is 'caught' from the linguistic environment. It must be noted that often in our ordinary speech there is a longer pause between two separate sounds in a single word than there is between two or three words forming a common phrase. Therefore a child will often hear a phrase as a single word and treat it as such, like that rather older child than the one we have been concerned with who wrote that she did not like 'gozinta sums', meaning division sums— 'goes into'. So, in hearing and treating phrases in this way, the child is learning something of the grammatical units of the mother tongue; words run together in speech in this way belong together as grammatical units. The study of the syntax of a language is the study of which word goes with which and along with that goes the more minor study of the forms the words take when they stand in a particular relationship to another word or words. Here, too, is something that the child begins to 'catch' from the linguistic environment. A child accustomed to seeing her father smoking a pipe was surprised one day to see him with a cigarette in his mouth. Her comment was: 'Daddy's piping a cigarette!' The interesting thing about the comment is that the child would never have heard the word 'pipe' used in that particular way; the normal sound-patterns of the sentences had taken over and fitted the form of the word to these accustomed patterns. There is no suggestion that the child was even aware that she had added 'ing' to the word 'pipe'; but the least that can be said is that there had been formed the linguistic habit of adding 'ing' to certain words when they occurred in a particular kind of sequence.

But how does the child use this rapidly increasing vocabulary? The child, like that adult, is not always using language for the same purpose. 'Good morning' has a different purpose from 'Pass the salt', and the 'please' which usually follows 'Pass the salt' is different in its purpose from both, though in that context it is nearer to 'Good morning' than to the direct request that the salt should be passed. Investigators usually classify children's speech according to the purpose for which it is used, or, more accurately perhaps, since the child is generally unaware of his purposes, according to the results which the use of the language achieves. Some terms that the student of this aspect of language will meet in the literature on the subject are: manipulative, declarative, synpractic, egocentric, and socialised.

The terms *manipulative* and *declarative* are used by Lewis. The former term indicates the use of language by the child in order to get someone to do something for him; the latter refers to the use of speech that arouses an expression of feeling on the part of another person.

The term *synpractic* is translated from the Russian of Vigotsky who drew attention to the use of language by the child in such a way as to help him with something he is trying to achieve by himself or as a kind of commentary running parallel to an activity as, for example, when the child is doing a simple jigsaw puzzle and says as he fits the pieces together: 'This one goes here and that one goes there!'

The terms *egocentric* and *socialised* are Piaget's broad divisions. His emphasis on the egocentricity of children's speech aroused considerable controversy, for no one had previously made so much of this aspect of children's speech. In egocentric speech the child is not concerned with other people and it does not matter to him whether what he says is being listened to or not. Yet Piaget does include in egocentric speech talking for the pleasure of associating with the activity of the moment anyone who happens to be present and some writers, notably Charlotte Buhler, would not regard speech of that kind as being truly egocentric but rather as expressing a need, the social need, for contact with other people. Nevertheless such speech is different from socialised speech as Piaget defined it, for he limited the term to speech in which the child is deliberately addressing someone, trying to get that other person to do something or even merely say something in answer to a question. Vigotsky also found himself at odds with Piaget on the question of egocentric speech. As we have seen, he placed great emphasis on the idea expressed by the term 'synpractic'—speech related to some practical activity and aiding the performance of it. He ascribed to this kind of speech a most important function in the development of the child. He saw it as a transitional step between overt and silent thinking. 'Synpractic' speech, he maintained, was a necessary step towards the inner or subvocal speech which accompanies most of our mental activity. Most of us at one time or other in our adult life find ourselves indulging in 'synpractic' speech. We encounter a problem with elements that are difficult to sort out and find that if we speak aloud we can get the focus clearer. It may be added, too, that the writing down of the working out of a problem is a more elaborate form of 'synpractic' speech in which we use 'speech made visible' in addition to the sub-vocal speech with which it is accompanied.

Much of the discussion that has gone on about the functions of language in childhood has been a discussion of the definition of terms. Yet certain aspects of the use children make of the meanings in language that they have acquired have been universally observed. It is the categorising of these that arouses discussion. These functions are:

1. In Samuel Butler's phrase, language 'lengthens the arm'. The child discovers that by means of his voice he is able to get things done that he could not do himself, e.g. get hold of a toy that is physically out of his reach.

2. Calling attention to his needs.

3. Calling attention to himself. He may be speaking about something quite outside himself but really be interested in directing attention towards himself. Or it may be a direct request: 'Watch me' as he does something in order to receive praise for something accomplished.

4. Thinking aloud. 'Synpractic' speech as in the example of the jigsaw puzzle.

5. Verbal play. The child seems to enjoy the sound of his own voice and the rhythm of words. He invents words on the analogy of words already known. Nursery rhymes give him pleasure. The rich collections made of counting-out rhymes and game-rhymes as in the work of the Opies indicate how important a role the 'singing' aspect of words plays in the development of the child's social life among his peers.

6. Allied to this is the invention not only of words but of persons. Imaginary playmates are characteristic features of childhood. These playmates not only are people for lonely children to speak to; they also perform the very useful

function of bearing the blame when something goes wrong: 'Look what Dobbie's done! He's a silly donk! But he didn't mean it.'

7. Satisfying curiosity. Why this? and Why that? At one stage the curiosity seems to be more about words than about things and this accounts for the great upward surge of vocabulary that follows the first realisation that things have names.

These various functions of language, though theoretically separable and identifiable, are closely interwoven throughout a child's whole speech. Certainly in any one day all of these functions are likely to manifest themselves in the closely-woven pattern of the child's developing speech.

THE PRACTICAL ASPECT

For the teacher at work a knowledge of the various functions of language at the earlier stages of speech seems an obvious necessity, for these functions persist throughout life. At the least a knowledge of these functions is likely to give a teacher a surer basis, or a more confident basis, for interpreting what a child says—reading, as it were, beneath the words.

The idea of 'levels of meaning' has a special importance in the teaching situation, for 'levels of meaning' implies levels of experience—experience of the word as well as the thing in a variety of contexts. Adults in general—though teachers by the special nature of their contacts with children may be exceptions—show a curious indifference to the great gulf that lies between the child and the adult in the matter of experience. At the earliest stages of education the teacher should be alert to the possibility that a child's lack of understanding of a particular point may be due not to lack of intelligence on the child's part but to a lack of

E

realisation on her own part of just how slender a child's store of meanings may be.

A teacher was once telling a class about the cultivation of rice. He mentioned the 'channels' in the paddy-fields and it was only after he had finished his exposition and started asking and answering questions that he discovered that one or two children were puzzled by the word 'channel'. The only channel they had ever heard of until then was the English Channel and they found it extremely difficult to adjust the focus of the word to the new context while all the time other ideas were being pushed at them. If there is any significance for the teacher in the study how children acquire a meaningful vocabulary, it is that it is likely to foster the habit of thinking of the words as ancillary to the experience. The teacher who throws the word 'channel' casually into a talk to pupils without giving a thought to how the pupils could have come to have a meaning for the word is a very different and inferior kind of teacher to the one who is aware that possibly some of the children have actually crossed the English Channel and think of it as, perhaps, a stormy sea, that others may have played on the beaches and looked out over the Channel, while to others still the Channel may be a strip of blue separating England and France on the map.

Even simpler words than 'channel' sometimes demonstrate in a dramatic manner how necessary it is for the teacher to be aware of the experiences behind a child's use of words as well as of the experiences which he himself has come to regard as integral in the use of particular words. There is the curious instance of the young child who responded to a situation in an apparently very unenlightened manner until the teacher had a sudden insight which showed that it was she who, before the flash of insight, was acting in an unenlightened, and indeed mentally blind, manner. This happened during a re-examination of Piaget's number experiments with young children when the experimenter modified the experiments somewhat and interpolated a few questions as his own interest developed. He put two pennies on the table and asked how many there were. 'Two.' He took one of the pennies away and asked how many were left. 'One.' He put three pennies in a row on the table and asked how many there were on the table. 'Three.' He took one penny away and asked again how many were left. The answer this time was again, 'One.' So he went back again to the two-penny stage with the same questions and the same correct answers. He repeated the three-penny stage and again got the wrong answer to the question as to how many were left. It was only after he had tried the same with four pennies that he realised that the child's answers were all correct. The child had been speaking about the penny that *had* left in each case, not the pennies that *were* left behind on the table.

Concentrate on the experiences that give the words meaning, and misunderstanding is reduced. We as adults assume that the child understands his words as we understand them. But when misunderstanding and apparent slowness of learning occur, it will often be found that it is the adult's not the child's logic that is at fault. We arrive at a station and learn that the train *left* five minutes before. So we are *left* behind. In the one case 'left' applies to the thing that has gone; in the other to the thing that has not gone. Is it any wonder that the child finds the language sometimes confusing. Take another simple and common word—more. 'More' is often and rightly given as the opposite of 'less'. If you have more of something than somebody, he will have a smaller quantity of it. A child looking at two plates of porridge of the same size, one half-full and the other nearly full, will easily tell which one has more in it. But when that child, the plates having been emptied, is asked whether he wants more porridge and says he does, then his mother is almost certain to give him less. The child is unlikely to notice in the case of porridge, but he may be puzzled with sweets or biscuits. He already has had two, let us say, is asked whether he would like more and is given one.

The word 'another' has been known to cause confusion in a child's mind. A child given a sweet was, perhaps unnecessarily, asked if he would like another one. Surprisingly, he said no. But later he asked for more and began to cry when his mother merely said he should have accepted one when he had the chance. Owing to the accident of a particular context, that child had formed the idea that when he was asked if he would like another one he was merely being offered a different one and would have to surrender the one he already had.

Only by a close awareness of what is going on in a child's mind can a teacher be moderately sure of the meanings that are being aroused by her words and actions. This awareness can only be acquired by persistent observation, and often, no matter how closely the teacher attends to what lies behind the pupil's words and actions, she will still find herself puzzled by the results. A curious instance of 'misteaching' occurred during the writer's investigations into the perception of words by young children. An infant had been taught to recognise the words 'bus' and 'man' equally well and these were the only two printed words she was at that time able to recognise. The idea was to test the hypothesis that the outline shape of a word is one of the dominant features in recognition by substituting 'bun' for 'bus' at a particular point expecting the child to say 'bus', thus confirming the hypothesis. She said 'man', however, and when told it was not man she put her finger on the 'n' and insisted that it *was* man. Only on reflection was it realised that this child has been taught that 'n' was 'man' because, during the practice, 'man' had been written down frequently with the child looking on and it was when the pencil was completing the latter 'n' that the word 'man' was said.

Every experienced teacher in the course of his or her career encounters instances of the kind related here, and no doubt many similar misunderstandings occur without being noticed. The young teacher, however, who is keenly aware of the role of experience in the developing of a meaningful vocabulary will be in some measure fore-armed against misunderstandings and mis-communications.

Chapter 4

THINKING

HERE are two contrasting examples of thinking. The first comes from childhood, the second from adult life.

1. A child of three was a very keen listener to the BBC programme 'Listen with Mother' which was broadcast every day of the week except Saturday and Sunday at quarter to two. In the child's mind, the phrase 'quarter to two' had become strongly associated with 'Listen with Mother'. Often she would ask her mother to let her listen to 'Listen with Mother'. Almost as often her mother would look at the clock and say, 'It's not time yet. It does not come on until quarter to two.' Answers of this kind led naturally to questions. 'What's quarter to two?' and so on until after a time the child was able to 'read' quarter to two on the clock although no other position in the hands had any particular meaning for her except those positions that were drawing near to quarter to two. She had also discovered that the hands of the clock move though they can hardly be seen to move and, when the minute hand was leaving twenty minutes to two, would be able to say with conviction that it would soon be quarter to two.

One morning just after breakfast the clock stopped, but the fact that it had stopped was not noticed for some time. When the father noticed that the clock had stopped, he got the key, wound the clock up, and began to set it at the right time. Meanwhile the child looked on and asked the appropriate questions. What are you doing? Why are you doing it? and so on. After the operation had been completed, the child went outside to play. Soon afterwards she came back into the house and said to her father, 'Put the clock at quarter to two, and let's have "Listen with Mother".'

2. The driver of a car who was being held up on a rather narrow road by a lorry found himself looking at the details of the lorry, for there was little else he *could* see. As the vehicle went round a bend, he noticed a projecting flange on the front wheel like a smaller wheel about eighteen inches in diameter and concentric with the large wheel. This reminded him of days spent on a farm where there was a tractor with a wheel with a similar flange that had been used for driving a belt that in turn supplied power to a circular saw, a threshing-mill, or a corn-bruiser. It had been customary to jack up the rear wheel which had this belt-drive attachment and he remembered being given a sketchy set of reasons why it was possible for one back wheel to remain stationary on the ground while the other was driven round by the engine. The flange on the lorry wheel was not quite the shape that would take a driving belt, however, and, moreover, since it was on the front wheel and the lorry was not a front-wheel-drive type, that flange could hardly be used for driving a belt. And yet the wheels might have been changed round because of wear on the tyres. He was still trying to fit the flange into a logical pattern when the lorry turned off on to a side-road and he then began to think of other things, though he still had no solution to the little problem. Some time later something in a conversation brought the matter back to his mind again. 'By the way,' he said, 'have you ever noticed a kind of flange on the wheels of heavy lorries?' 'Yes,' was the reply. 'What are they for?' 'You've obviously never hitch-hiked,' was the reply. 'You try getting into the cab of one of these lorries without the help of that step!'

These two examples in their different ways illustrate

certain aspects of normal thought. What is perhaps first noticeable in both instances is that both are working with analogies. 'You can't argue from analogy,' is a very common caution in logic, but the answer to it is 'Can you point to any other way?' It all depends on the particular analogy, for the only way of finding a solution to a problem is to look at past experiences and select from them the one which is appropriately analogous. The one that is appropriately analogous is that which 'fills the gap'.

The first example shows the child as a logical being. The child's request to put the clock at quarter to two so that the radio could be switched on to have 'Listen with Mother' is logically perfect *within the child's experience*. Until she saw her father move the hands of the clock, she had had no experience that would have told her the hands could be moved at will. All her previous experience had led her to take it for granted that the hands of the clock simply went round. She thought no more about it than she did about the sun rising in the morning; it happened, and until that day it had never ceased to happen. Part of the constellation of experiences was that from the radio when it was switched on, if the hands of the clock had reached quarter to two, 'Listen to Mother' would be heard. Into this situation came the surprising new fact that her father could move the hands of the clock. So he could put them at quarter to two and then, if he switched on the radio, one could have 'Listen with Mother'. This is the same kind of thinking that led people to believe the earth was flat and that the earth was the centre round which the sun, moon and stars revolved. What was lacking, what led to the false conclusion, was not lack of logic, not even in this case lack of words, but lack of the experience that would have prevented the false conclusion from being drawn. It is often said that 'the child has a logic of his own' implying that the child thinks very differently from the adult. It would be extremely difficult, however, to find any case of thinking by a child which will not on examination be found to fit into the framework of ordinary logic, no matter how fanciful it might seem. Often indeed it is the very directness of the logic which gives the thought the appearance of fancifulness. A child had been told that you could see if somebody liked butter by holding a butter-cup under that person's chin: if the yellow of the butter-cup showed on his skin then that person liked butter. A day or two later he was holding a buttercup under a black retriever's chin to see if it liked butter. All delightfully fanciful? Or merely a logical extension of the adult's fancy? As the child did not himself believe either of them as far as could be discovered, it seems likely that he was merely using logic to beat the adults at their own game.

The second example is an instance of simple failure in thinking on the part of an adult. Here we have an example both of how an analogy may interfere with a process of thought because it was not the appropriate analogy and also of how the appearance of a thing may set the mind on a false trial. It has been noted earlier with reference to Piaget's work that the child's thinking may be tyrannised by the appearance of things. Here we have this same tyranny blocking the thinking of an adult. Having noted the resemblance between the flange on the lorry wheel and that of the tractor, he assumed a similarity of function. Had this train of thought not exerted so great a pressure, he might have noted something about the flange that would have led him towards the right answer, for these flanges are not smooth like belt-pulleys but 'bramble-marked' as steps sometimes are to prevent slipping. A circular step of any kind, however, was not within his experience; the bramble-markings failed to suggest the appropriate analogy and so the answer to the problem was not forthcoming.

The work of Jean Piaget has had very considerable influence in recent years upon educational thought in Britain, though much less in America. Piaget employs a highly technical language with the result that his writings make difficult reading for the non-specialist. There is also the added difficulty that he does not always keep his terms constant in their meanings. The student, therefore, who finds Piaget difficult to understand may comfort himself with the thought that nearly all serious commentators on his work have felt it necessary to confess that they have found him very difficult to follow too.

Fortunately, the main direction of Piaget's thought is comparatively easy to follow. Besides, his works contain a great store of examples of children's speech in a large variety of situations and no one who reads these can fail to be stimulated towards a re-appraisal of his thinking about the nature of thought in the child.

On the basis of observation and experiment spread over many years Piaget came to the conclusion that there were five fairly clearly marked phases in the development of thinking ability in the human being. These phases are:

1. *From birth to 2 years.* A phase that may be termed 'thoughtless' in the sense that the child can perform only motor actions. This does not mean, however, an absence of intelligent behaviour, for the beginnings of intelligent behaviour are observable in such activities as the development of the idea that an object covered up by a cloth can be reached by removing the cloth—an achievement which *develops* during this period. It is also a period in which the infant is learning the control and co-ordination of his bodily movements and in so doing becoming orientated in his immediate world. Parallel is the development and co-

ordination of his sense-impressions. Piaget designates this period as the Sensori-Motor Period.

2. *From 2 to 4 years.* Imitation is one of the main characteristics of this phase in the child's development. The imitation takes very frequently the form of pretending to do something, e.g. sleeping or to be something other than he is. Piaget ascribes to imitation an important role—that of being a step towards imagery. When the imitative actions are, in Piaget's term 'internalized', that is, take place in the mind only, then we have thinking in terms of images which is the genesis of symbolic behaviour. At the same time imitation plays an important part in the development of language. The child's language at this stage is highly egocentric. The main characteristic of this phase, however, is that the child is so greatly dependent upon the actual manipulation or physical presence of whatever it is he is thinking about. This phase is designated the phase of Pre-Operational Thought, but to see the force of this designation it is necessary to know what Piaget means by 'operation'. This is the term he uses to indicate 'internalised actions'—that is to say, solving a problem in the mind without having to manipulate objects externally. Although towards the end of this phase there are some indications that the child is becoming capable of operations in this sense, the ability develops slowly. Indeed according to Piaget, operational thinking does not become characteristic until about the eighth year and then in the form of 'concrete operations', another special term. There is, however, among the commentators on Piaget's work some little doubt as to what is precisely meant by 'concrete operations'. Lewis, for example, in *Language, Thought and Personality* (Harrap) writes, 'We have seen that he (Piaget) specifies this period of later childhood as the stage of concrete operations—meaning by this that the child can deal

with the observable features of a situation, whether actually present to his senses or imagined by him.' On the other hand Peel, in *The Pupil's Thinking* (Oldbourne) states: 'Concrete operations have a particular restriction in that they are carried out by children only with reference to objects and materials which are visibly and tangibly present.'

3. *4 to 7 years*. Of all Piaget's experiments those relating to this phase of development have had the greatest impact on the thought of educationists in this country, for here belong those experiments with beads and liquids that with minor variations have been repeated by scores of teachers and students throughout the country and have been demonstrated on television. Equal numbers of beads are put in two glasses of the same size and shape. The child readily admits that there is the same number of beads in each glass. The beads are then transferred from one of the glasses to another of a different shape. Thereupon the child maintains that the number of beads in that glass is no longer the same as the number in the untouched glass. The same is found when liquid is used—the quantity of liquid in the differently shaped glass is declared no longer to be the same. Or the child is shown two equal rows of beads—equal in number and equally spaced apart—and then the beads in one row are more widely separated so that the row is longer. The child then declares that the longer row has more beads in it. These judgements are denoted 'intuitive' by Piaget. The characteristic is that the perceptual aspect of the problem predominates; the line of beads looks longer, so there must be more beads in it. There is a failure to see more than one aspect of a complex situation. This is the phase of Intuitive Thought or Judgement.

4. *8 to 11 years*. This is the stage when the child can

perform concrete operations. As we have seen, there is some doubt among commentators on Piaget about the precise meaning of 'concrete operations', but whether the objects need to be visibly or tangibly present or not, certain new characteristics develop in the child's thinking. It is less dominated by the immediate perception. His thinking is now becoming structured. The word 'becoming' is important here, for there is no suggestion that there are sudden advances. On the contrary Piaget found that although at the age of 8 children may recognise that a ball of clay rolled out to a sausage shape has merely changed its shape with no change in the amount of clay in it, yet they will not admit that it has not changed in weight. He found that it was not until the age of eleven that they were able to see that in spite of a change in shape of that nature all three attributes of substance, weight and volume remained unaltered. That is to say the idea of 'conservation' was only gradually being extended to include the various attributes. The child's powers of generalisation have not fully developed. He is unable to formulate general principles from concrete instances. On the other hand he is now able to classify material, to place a series in order (e.g. sticks of differing lengths), to pair corresponding elements, and to form concepts of space and time. Such, in very brief, is the stage of Concrete Operations.

5. *11 to 14 years*. The phase of logical operations. During this phase the child begins to formulate hypotheses and to test them out. The concept of probability appears. That is to say, it is now possible for the child, now adolescent, to think within such a framework as: 'If such-or-such a thing were done, then one or other of the following results is likely to occur.' Thinking within a general structured framework is now possible.

One of the things the student of language is most likely to be aware of in reading the reports of Piaget's interviews with children is the persistence of the assumption on the part of the questioners that the children ought to have the same meaning for the terms in which the questions were couched as the questioners themselves had. But we have seen that in English a simple word like 'left' may lead to misunderstandings between adult and child. Is there any reason to suppose that the same thing does not happen in French spoken in Switzerland? In the Piaget experiments new experiences were continually being given to the children and the questions put to them were in language that referred specifically to the new situations, but there is no sign that account was taken of the previous experiences the children would have had *outside* the experimental situations. Had those children, for example, ever seen a conjurer producing a rabbit from a hat? Are Swiss children ever told the equivalent of the English fantasy about buttercups held under the chin? Do they ever hear the story about the porridge pot that would not stop boiling over and producing more and more porridge? And what about the way in which the Bible miracles are presented to them? The pressures of such stories and fantasies must surely bear upon the child's developing concepts of language in relation to reality. A considerable amount of work is still going on, however, in the field in which Piaget was so diligent a pioneer and it is possible that the modifications that a stricter attention to the linguistic context may enforce upon his theories may not imply a radical change in his general theory.

The two examples of thinking given at the beginning of this chapter may be taken as a limited comment on Piaget's work. How does the 3-year-old's request for 'Listen with Mother' fit into the Pre-Operational Phase in Piaget's

theory of development? Certainly it was connected with
the concrete situation, the visible moving of the hands of
the clock. But the request came after the hands had been
moved, indeed after the child had gone outside to play.
Nor had the child herself handled the clock. Furthermore
the radio that had to be switched on was in another room.
So certainly in this case there is no question of the objects
being present, visible and tangible. The thinking in this
case, however, is 'concrete' in the sense that it is concerned with a specific situation concerning real objects.
What Piaget's theory would not allow, or at least would
not encourage, is the interpretation given earlier in the
chapter, namely that the child here in her limited way was
doing the same kind of thinking that led adults to think
that the world was flat. Nor does the Piagetian theory encourage the thought that it was limitation of experience
(including the verbal experience to go with the actual experience) rather than lack of logic which led the child to
the wrong conclusion. The second example, too, has its
point in connection with Piaget's work. For here we have
an adult—who in other ways had shown himself to be
a reasonably intelligent adult—indulging in 'intuitive
thought' or at least in the kind of thinking Piaget found to
be characteristic of the 4 to 7 year-olds, thinking that was
dominated by the perceptual aspect of the object about
which his cerebration was taking place. Another puzzling
aspect of Piaget's work is his treatment of classification
which he regards as typical of the 8 to 11 age range. And
yet, as we have already seen, the very fact of acquiring a
vocabulary involves the beginnings of classification. Early
examples of classifying words are *tree* and *flower*, but even
the narrower word 'dog' has a classifying function since
dogs are of many different sizes, shapes, and colours. It is
noticeable, however, that in the list of words used by a

3-year-old on one particular day there is only one strongly classifying word—*clothes*.

Earlier in this book it was suggested that 'finding the thing that fits' appears to be a natural tendency in human beings and that the actual finding is accompanied by a feeling of satisfaction. This idea is closely allied to that expressed by Sir Frederic Bartlett in his study, *Thinking*, where he uses the phrase 'filling the gaps'.

The word 'thinking' is, of course, used in ordinary speech with many different meanings. Negatively, it may be synonymous with 'forgetting' as in 'I just can't think of the name at the moment'. It may be synonymous with 'day-dreaming' as in 'She lay lazily thinking about the holiday she had planned'. It may be used as part of an exclamation as in 'What do you think!' The kind of thinking we are concerned with in this chapter is, however, thinking of a more positive kind, the thinking that is carried out by the housewife when she is trying to organise her shopping in such a way as to meet the family needs on the one hand and not overspend the house-keeping allowance on the other. Or the kind of thinking the garage mechanic has to do when he is tracing a fault in an engine. To some extent also we shall be concerned with the kind of thinking the poet or novelist engages in, although that aspect of language is specially considered in a later chapter.

In *Thinking* Bartlett describes four main types of thinking: mathematical and logical thinking, experimental thinking associated with experimental science, everyday thinking, and the artist's thinking. He is willing to admit that these may not be the only kinds of thinking, suggesting that religious or mystical thinking may on investigation be found to have characteristics which the other

kinds do not possess and that the study of legal thinking
might show that this is also in various ways an independent
kind.

In his book three of the types of thinking he discusses
come under the heading 'adventurous thinking'. The one
which does not come under that heading is mathematical
and logical thinking which comes under the heading of
'thinking within closed systems'. It is the 'closed' type of
thinking that he discusses first, after an introduction in
which he suggests that much may be learned about the
nature of thinking by examining its similarity to the practise
of a physical skill.

The simplest example of a closed system is the numerical series. The kind of thinking that may be required to be
done in connection with such a series is that which will
lead to the correct filling of a gap within the series, i.e.
interpolation

o   3   6   9   .   .   18   21

or an extension of the given series:

o   3   6   9   12   15   .   .

Here the terms are clearly defined; all the information
is present that will enable the gaps to be filled with no
doubt as to their precision of fit; there are no branching
possibilities, and nothing will be discovered that will
change the significance of the terms.

The examples given here are of the very simplest, but it
must not therefore be taken that 'closed-system' thinking
is the easiest kind of thinking. It is simple only in the sense
that it is the kind of thinking which is easiest to describe.

Bartlett's description of the thinker in the closed system
runs as follows:

The thinker in the closed system is in the position of con-
templating a finished structure. Very often this may be
exceedingly complex and elaborate and the rules of its con-

F

struction difficult to appreciate. The thinker is, however, in the position of a spectator searching for something which he must treat as being in some way 'there' all the time. His search is rational but it is often emotionally sustained, and if it is, the emotion is appropriate to that which is associated with the contemplation of form and beauty of form, and is aesthetic or akin to the aesthetic.

In schools, perhaps ever since anything that could be called a school existed, the emphasis when it has not been on rote-learning has been on thinking of the 'closed' type. The pupil in the days of Classical predominance spent the greater part of his time trying to elicit meanings that were already 'there' as complete as the author could make them. It was 'closed' thinking on a grander scale that Bacon was rebelling against in *The Advancement of Learning* when he urged scholars to rid themselves of the fantasy that a thing must be so because in this or that ancient author it was said to be so, to cast out the idea that knowledge was to be found in the writings of the Ancients and set about the experimental study of the world about them. And one of the most powerful influences on the practise of education in the twentieth century—the standardised test—has given a very firm rooting to the idea that thinking within closed systems is the kind of thinking that a school should most concern itself with. This development has been perhaps a matter of expedience growing out of the simple fact that tests consisting of questions of the 'closed system' type are far and away the easiest to mark—one right word or numeral, one tick.

We turn again to Bartlett.

It is when he is summarising his discussion of thinking in experimental science that he draws an explicit contrast between thinking within closed systems and 'adventurous thinking':

The experimental thinker is in the position of somebody who must use whatever tools may be available for adding to some structure that is not yet finished, and that he himself is certainly not going to complete. Because the materials that he must use have properties of their own, many of which he cannot know until he uses them, and some of which in all likelihood are actually generated in the course of their use, he is in the position of an explorer rather than that of a spectator. His thinking, too, is often emotionally sustained, and if it is, the emotion is one of those appropriate to the chase, to risk, to adventure, and to sport.

He does not suggest, however, that all thinking in the experimental sciences is of this adventurous kind. On the contrary he states that the progress of experimental science

is made up essentially by a very small number of original inquiries, which may be widely separated, followed, as a rule, by a very large number of routine inquiries. The most important feature of original experimental thinking is the discovery of overlap and agreement where formerly only isolation and difference were recognised.

He goes on to say that in most fields of enquiry a stage is reached at which routine thinking comes near to wearing itself out by utilising a limited range of techniques to establish more and more minute and specialised detail. At the same time, however, possibly in some other science or in another branch of the same science, new techniques of enquiry are being developed (e.g. based on more accurate measuring instruments) and then 'an original mind, never wholly contained in any one conventionally enclosed field of interest . . . seizes upon the possibility that there may be some unsuspected overlap, takes the risk whether there is or not, and gives the old subject-matter a new look.'

When he comes to deal with everyday thinking, Bartlett sees its distinguishing characteristic as assertiveness. In

closed system thinking, the compulsion to achieve completion, to fill the gap, is, he says, in the nature of the
system itself. The same is true of the thinking of the experimental scientist; there is a goal to be achieved and the
goal is inherent in the relations of the material he is working with; so here too there is a compulsion to go on that
derives not from the scientist's own nature but from the
nature of the materials and their internal relationships. In
what he calls 'everyday thinking' there is not this compulsion outside the thinker; its source is now within the
thinker and his social group. In seeking to claim 'necessity'—i.e. logical inevitability—everyday thinking resorts
to assertiveness and when contradictory issues claim the
same necessity, then the only way either side has of en-
forcing its claim is yet more violent assertiveness.

While discussion of the aesthetic aspect of language is
properly the concern of a later chapter in this book, it is fitting to include at this stage a note about Bartlett's view of
the artist's thinking. This I do by appropriate quotation:

The broad strategy of the artist's thinking is neither to
compel by proof nor to convince by assertiveness; but to
satisfy by attainment . . . the requirements of a standard. In
the attainment that it reaches there remains something personal
to the artist, but also there is something common to all who
will accept or can appropriate the standard. The artist's
tactics are to prepare the materials which he finds through his
observation, not accepting them as other thinkers may do, but
working them into the form most fit for his medium and his
ultimate design; and then, perhaps with sudden leaps here and
there to make a succession of steps to a terminus which is the
artist's particular expression of his standard in terms of the
materials he has chosen to use. The step sequence which he
effects is never one which converges steadily to a single issue.
In its earlier stages every step opens up more diverging paths.
Later, characteristically, it reaches some critical stage beyond

which each successive step achieves a partial issue which presents itself as the one that is most satisfying but never as the
only possible one.

Bartlett is one of the more attractive writers on this subject and that is one of the reasons why I have paid this
amount of attention to this book of his. It is only too easy
in looking for information about what experts think about
thinking to find oneself with a book which is largely incomprehensible to anyone without a specialist training in
logic and psychology. Bartlett makes as few demands upon
the reader as is consistent with a serious and informed
treatment of the subject.

There is another aspect of this book and also of his
easier *The Mind at Work and Play* (Allen & Unwin) which
makes his work valuable to teachers. It is that the experiments he describes are of a kind to suggest the use of
similar experiments in the class-room. The idea of carrying out such experiments would not be the discovery of
new truths or even the further buttressing of old truths
but the providing of material inside the class-room for the
discussion of how we think based on the pupils' own experimental efforts.

Another aspect of Bartlett's work which gives it a
special relevance to education at the present time is his
emphasis on 'adventurous thinking'. At no time does he
say in so many words that adventurous thinking is to be
encouraged; he does not even say that it *can* be encouraged, but his feeling that it both ought and can be encouraged comes through between the lines of the two books
referred to.

It is a remarkable fact that writers about thinking so
often appear to be unable to avoid ambiguity. The ambi-
guities and obscurities of Piaget, already noted, are monumental; even Bartlett's so much more perspicuous writing

is not free from shifts of meaning that give rise to a certain mistiness in the communication. 'Thinking within closed systems' shifts towards 'routine thinking' and, while never quite becoming routine thinking entirely, acquires that aura. Similarly 'adventurous thinking' veers towards 'original thinking'. At the same time it seems rather odd to find 'everyday thinking' with its assertiveness classed under 'adventurous thinking' with its inclination towards originality. Bruner, another expert investigator into the nature and technique of thinking, regarded Bartlett's *Thinking* as a pioneer work which might have an important influence on later work in this field. At the same time Bartlett's insistence upon adventurousness led Bruner to compare his attitude to that of an Elizabethan buccaneer.

My reason for paying so much attention to Piaget and Bartlett when writing about such a ranging subject as thinking is that these two writers are probably more frequently mentioned than any others when this topic is being discussed in the context of education. And yet some other writer dealing with this topic might well branch out into learning theory. In this book I assume on the part of the reader a certain basic acquaintance with the mechanisms of learning. Much of the basic work in that branch of knowledge has been carried out with non-linguistic creatures like octopi and rats, if not transistorised machines. Here, however, I am concerned in general with the application of a theory of signs and signification to the teaching-learning situation, a very different thing from any non-linguistic process.

In my next chapter I shall be dealing specifically with the relationship between language and thought, but there are some related matters that are more conveniently dealt with here since they may be regarded as a comment on Bartlett's view of thinking as 'filling the gaps'.

What is the gap to be filled with? In the case of the numerical series from which certain terms have been omitted, there is no doubt that the gap will be filled by a number or numbers written down in the same convention as are those given in the series. In the case of problems like the one about the flange on the lorry wheel, the gap had to be filled by an analogous experience. Since to every experience there is a series of analogous experiences, it is a matter of selecting the one that fits. There are indeed two general types of difficulty in problem-solving:

(a) The difficulty of being unable to discern among all the analogous experiences recalled one which seems to come anywhere near filling the gap; they all seem to belong somewhere else.

(b) The difficulty of finding a number of seemingly appropriate analogies each of which, however, clashes with some other.

The flange on the lorry wheel is seen to be analogous to the flange on the tractor wheel.

The flange on the tractor wheel, however, has its own series of analogies e.g. belt-pulley.

The belt-pulley analogy is fed back and found not to fit.

The 'bramble-markings' on the lorry-flange are analogous to markings on steps. Pre-occupation with the other analogies, however, prevents this one being discerned.

It is a pity that the term 'analogy' is so often associated with weakness in argument (for example, 'You can't drive the analogy too far'), because this suggests that there is some other way of thinking of greater intrinsic validity. If there is, I have not been able to find it in print or talk. An analogy is not a mere 'figure of speech', the 'extended metaphor' of the old-style English composition books; that is indeed one of the forms the analogical process takes. But another form is to be found in the extremely elaborate simulation programmes of, say, space-research where astronomical sums of money (i.e. enormous amounts of time and energy) are devoted to the creation of situations as strongly analogous as possible to the situations that previous analogies have shown to be likely to be met by astronauts.

Underneath it all is the fact that language cannot be other than analogical since it is the record of analogical experiences. No two objects are identical, yet often we give them the same name thereby recording the likenesses.

THE PRACTICAL ASPECT

It cannot be too strongly stressed that a teacher cannot be too consistently aware of the difference between his or her experience of things, of words, and of words in relation to things and the experience of the pupils.

A good general principle to hold on to is that if a pupil does not understand what he is being told, then the likelihood is that it is not the pupil who is dull but the explanation which assumes more experience of things and of words than the pupil possesses. All the words used may be simple, but they may not all be used in the way the child has experienced them. One word misunderstood in this way may set a pupil thinking on quite the wrong lines.

The fact that there are these differences is one of the main reasons for the copious use of visual aids—and yet at the same time the discreet use. One of the things that has emerged in recent years more clearly than ever before is the value of the model. Models are by no means merely children's playthings. Any museum with a maritime section will show that the construction of accurate models has been found necessary in ship-building for many a long day, the model here being not a copy but a miniature prototype. There is hardly a branch of human activity today where the

making of models is not a major part of the preliminary
work in construction or regarded as necessary for explanation. The design of aircraft wings, for example, is the result of large numbers of experiments in wind-tunnels that
cost hundreds of thousands of pounds to erect, run and
maintain; no school of chemistry would regard itself as
complete without some elaborate models of molecular
structures; a great deal of information about the working
of the nervous system has been discovered by the construction of transistorised models of simple nerve-circuits.

The implication is not that a large part of the pupils'
time should be spent in the making of models. The construction of an elaborate Norman castle, for example,
might not bring with it either enough knowledge or sense
of history to justify the time taken in its construction.
What I am suggesting is that the picture, the model or the
diagram are essential in the process of communication for
the plain reason that words without reference to the things
they signify are meaningless and of all the senses the visual
is educationally the most important.

It is not surprising that the 'draw a man' test has been
taken as one of the tests of intelligence at the younger
levels, for in drawing a man a child has to reason out
spatial relationships in an actual object (or picture) and
transfer them in a new form to paper.

The diagram is the step between the actual object or the
picture and the word, for the diagram is more abstract than
the picture and its abstractions is of a different kind from
that of the word even at the label level. A diagram may indeed summarise the meaning of a word, e.g. the simple
outline drawing of two wings and a fuselage standing for
an aeroplane.

Chapter 5

LANGUAGE AND THOUGHT

CAN we think without words? At some time or other that question will come up in any prolonged discussion of language. Very long and very wordy arguments have taken place about whether words are really necessary for thinking. There may have been wordless arguments too, but they will have taken place only after the wordy ones have reached an emotional climax. Yet overt discussion and argument are not the only kinds of thinking. People think without speaking very much oftener than they—figuratively speaking perhaps—speak without thinking. At any rate the question of the relationship between language and thought has been for a very long time discussed. Even the early behaviourist view that all thought is inner speech, which thirty years ago was thought by large numbers of people to be the really up-to-date point of view, had been in Plato's mind, for he said that when we are thinking the soul is speaking to itself. At the opposite pole in this matter was Galton who maintained that in his actual thinking he did not employ words. He claimed that he could not feel sure that he had really grasped a problem until he had 'disembarrassed it of words'. Earlier Berkeley had said that words were the great impediment to thought, but he never claimed that he could think without this impediment. On the other hand in his *Outline of Philosophy* Bertrand Russell wrote, "Almost all higher intellectual activity is a matter of words to the nearly total exclusion of everything else.'

This, is seems, was not the view of Einstein who, in a

discussion which Wertheimer, the Gestalt psychologist, reported in his *Productive Thinking* (Hamilton), maintained that language did not play any part in his thought-processes. He described the process of thinking in his own case as 'combinatory and associative play' in which there were 'visual and muscular elements'. It was only after this 'play' was over that he found himself engaged in a laborious search for words in order to communicate his thought.

So here we have Einstein and Russell, two eminent mathematicians, making apparently flatly contradictory statements about the relationship between language and thought: on the one hand words unnecessary for the actual thinking and only being called upon for communicating the end-result and on the other hand thinking at the higher levels being regarded as words and hardly anything else. Is this a real contradiction or merely an apparent one? In either case how is it to be resolved?

If we examine the functioning of language in a context where absolute precision of statement is possible, we may get a clearer picture of the process about which Einstein and Russell had such very different things to say. Such a context is the game of chess. It is, fortunately, not necessary for any reader of this book to be able to play chess in order to follow the simple steps of this argument.

There is no doubt that if you knew the rules of chess and had a chess-board and men in front of you, you could teach someone to play the game without using a word either in speech or writing. It would indeed be an interesting exercise in communication to do so. It is equally certain that if you did use words your teaching would be more effective and would take a much shorter time. On the other hand, without a chess-board and chess-men in front of you, either in fact or in diagram, you would find it an almost impossible task to teach anyone to play no matter how many words you used.

What part is language playing in such a context?

If you have the chess-board in front of you, you can place one of the chess-men on it and described with a running commentary of words the rules that govern the move of that particular chess-man. Moreover, you can do this against a background of knowledge about the purpose of the game which you have also communicated by means of language. That language will depend for its effectiveness on the drawing of appropriate analogies by the learner from his past experience. The words 'win', 'move', 'capture' and so on will convey meaning to him only if he has experienced them in association with situations fittingly parallel to those you are trying to explain to him. What your words are enabling him to do is to bring out of his past experience certain fairly general ideas and rearrange them in a new pattern, e.g. if he knows the game of draughts he will have a set of ideas against which to set the new ones. He will be helped in this case by the resemblance between the two games but hindered by their differences. One thing you will not do in teaching him the game is to give him a name for each one of the 64 squares, for if you were to do so you would confuse him with too many words. What happens is that he gets from you a series of general statements about the way in which each chess-man moves (e.g. the king moves one square at a time in any direction). Then when he is playing the game himself he sees on the board itself the particular squares the king can move to from any particular position. There is no need for him to name the squares even to himself. Is he then thinking without words? A beginner certainly uses words; he may sometimes be heard murmuring to himself: 'If I go there, he'll go there, and then . . .' The word 'there' has a precise meaning, however, only because the board is there in front of him and it is not a communicative word unless particular squares are actually pointed to. In the play of experts, however, language is discarded; it is one of the characteristics of the really first-class chess-players to be able to *visualise* the movement of the pieces and pawns in all the complexity of large numbers of combinations to the extent indeed as to be able to play several games without seeing the board.

It is indeed in the playing of 'blindfold' chess that we have the situation that elucidates Einstein's view of the role of language most effectively. In playing such a game the expert needs no words in the first place to tell him where the chess-men are before the game begins. He *sees* them mentally. He receives an announcement about his opponent's move in the form of words which tell him which pawn has been moved and into which square. He translates that move into a mental image of the board, visualises a reply and then translates that into language communicating his move thereby to his 'seeing' opponent who makes the appropriate move *in fact* on the chess-board—and so all through the game the expert is, like Einstein, using words only for communicating and receiving communications. His actual thinking is a matter of 'combinatory and associative play' in which there are 'visual and muscular' elements.

Two things need to be noted here, however: first, the kind of thinking that goes on in the playing of chess is thinking of a very narrow kind in the sense that though the combinations in the game are extremely complicated each move whether real or potential is limited in a precise manner by a set of conventions; second, the kind of thinking Einstein appears to have been referring to in his conversation with Wertheimer was his thinking as a mathematician where again the thinking is on paths prescribed by a set of conventions.

But how does this idea of the relationship between language and thought stand alongside the apparently opposite view held by Bertrand Russell that almost all higher intellectual activity is a matter of words to the nearly total exclusion of everything else?

To begin answering this question we need to go to no higher an intellectual activity than elementary arithmetic. How many letters are there in this line of print? You cannot tell without running rapidly, though not necessarily a step at a time, up a scale of words, for the size of a group that can be apprehended instantly is extremely small. The actual number-words in primitive languages is believed to be no more than *one, two, three*, a larger group than that being referred to merely by a word similar in meaning to our *many*. Since we cannot instantly perceive so small a number as, say, seventeen with precision, we cannot therefore visualise precisely that number of objects. Yet we can think of such a group because we have devised a scale of words for the measurement of quantity.

If there were no spaces between printed words and each letter were the same width, then we could tell at a glance which of two lines of print had the greater number of letters in it, but we could not say precisely how many letters there were in either of them without taking these verbal steps up the number-scale. It would be merely a case of perceiving that one line is longer than the other. It is not often in real life, however, that a comparison of quantities is so easily carried out. Even if we take such a simple matter as deciding how much sugar will be required for an Antarctic expedition, the sugar itself, the time, and the number of men involved are merely the starting-point of the calculations. During the calculations themselves nothing but the number-words are involved. After these have been manipulated, the result is applied to the actual sugar. But no real thing need be involved. There is no need for any reference to anything other than number-words themselves for it to be decided whether such a statement as $7,982 \times 12 = 95,784$ is true or not.

That paragraph is not an argument for regarding arithmetic as divorced from real things; it is merely part of a statement showing that Russell's statement about higher intellectual activity being a matter of words and hardly anything else can be shown to have a certain substance without scaling any formidable intellectual heights. But all higher intellectual activity is surely not confined to mathematics and Russell deliberately says 'almost all higher intellectual activity'. So we must take it that he has other things than mathematics in mind. With little modification, however, the principle still holds. The principle is that starting with observed facts and following on by means of analogies one can go far beyond any set of observed facts and move in a world of relationships signified by words. The whole number-system, for example, appears to be based upon very few facts of perception: a single item is distinguishable from no item at all, two items are distinguishable from a single item, a group of three items is distinguishable from a group of two, and with varying degrees of accuracy larger groups are distinguishable from these and from other larger groups. Upon these few facts of observation the whole vast number-system and its ramifications is erected—like a great inverted pyramid with very little contact with the world of ordinary perception.

If we leave the world of number and turn to words that are normally called 'abstract', we find a similar process taking place. If we take such a word as 'justice' and try to trace the origins of the idea behind the word, we find very different pictures. On the one hand there are a number of diverse theological views rooted in the idea of justice as God-given; on the other hand there are philosophers of different schools who in one way or another would trace the origins of the idea of justice back to a set of ideas that can be grouped under the phrase 'enlightened self-interest' or, less harshly, to the Christian rule—'Do unto others as you would that they should do unto you.' And yet how often do we hear the statement: 'There is no justice in the world' or, 'There's some justice in the world after all.' Such statements are an indication that it does not require a training in philosophical argument to lead one to the conclusion that the 'justice' has not the same sort of reality as the things which compose the material framework of our lives. Indeed many of the observed facts of daily life run counter to the idea of justice—one child is born deformed and a brother or sister born quite normal—how can the mother see justice in this situation? Or a mother of three small children is struck down with an incurable illness—what is *just* about that? Justice, we say, is an ideal that is never wholly attainable. So the content of the word is not such as can be pointed to with any certainty in the world of real events. In a sense, then, we have here more confirmation of Russell's point of view of the predominance of words in the higher intellectual activities.

That is to say, justice is not a *thing* that exists any more than Plato's Republic or More's Utopia existed. It is a word denoting a set of relationships which it is thought desirable should exist and which human beings, or some of them, work towards. This term then has a rather tenuous connection with things as they are—except in some of its narrower applications as in the appellation 'Justice of the Peace'—and gives further backing to Russell's statement about 'words and hardly anything else'.

When those statements by Einstein and Russell are looked at more broadly, however, they may be seen to be less contradictory than at first appears. The chess-master would not be able to play chess at all, with or without words, if his powers of perception, visualisation and reasoning had not been developed by the contact with other minds that language brings and by the contact with his own past experience in which language plays so great a part, and the same is true of Einstein. Einstein spoke about requiring language merely in order to communicate the results of his thinking, but he too was dependent on the language of others for the development of his ability to carry out that kind of thinking. Moreover, although it is true that 'communicate' normally means 'telling someone else' it is also true that thinking is very often a process of communicating with ourselves. We assimilate a new experience by telling ourselves how it stands in relation to a past experience and even though we may have no intention of communicating a conclusion we have reached to any other person, we are likely to sum it up in a formula of words for our own future reference. It is highly unlikely that even Einstein pursued a line of thought without reference to such summaries of past conclusions.

With Russell we have the other side of the medal complicated somewhat by a slight ambiguity and it is the ambiguity we shall have to deal with first. It lies in his use of 'word'. He implies that it is possible for a word to be a word even though it does not stand for anything other than itself. True, political speeches are often dismissed as 'mere words' implying that they are merely sound and fury signifying nothing. This situation, of course, could not arise unless the sounds that in such speeches signified nothing did signify something in other contexts. But Russell was referring to 'higher intellectual activity' and in this context words cannot be regarded as words unless they stand for something other than themselves—i.e. unless they are symbols. The question then is what are they symbols of? We have seen the answer in connection with the word 'justice'. Such words are symbols of sets of ideas derived from the observation of reality but proceeding by a series of analogies far beyond reality. It is only in a sense therefore that they can be said to be 'words and hardly anything else'; in another sense that 'hardly anything else' is of very great importance indeed. Words like 'honour', 'justice', and 'freedom' have played a far greater part in moving the forces of history than words which have a closer and more specific connection with real things. Such words in various subtle ways arouse emotional responses— and these are not only in themselves felt to be real but also result in action in relation to real things.

A thinker whose ideas have a direct bearing on these matters is Korzybski, an eccentric character whose book *Science and Sanity* has gradually come to be regarded as much more worthy of serious consideration than it was accorded during its first few years of existence. The usual descriptions given to this book by academic writers, if they mentioned it at all, was that it was the product of messianic delusion. They did not say so in so many words but they seldom left any doubt that that was what was to be inferred. In his recent book *Semantics* (Blackwell), however, Professor Stephen Ullman refers to

Science and Sanity as 'monumental' and so it may be that for all his eccentricity Korzybski is gradually becoming respectable.

Science and Sanity has never been published in Britain; it was one of Korzybski's eccentricities that he did not have his work published in the normal way. Instead he published it through an Institute of General Semantics established for the purpose of spreading his ideas. There is, however, a summary of Korzybski's ideas in Stuart Chase's *Tyranny of Words* and a lengthier simplification of them in *Language and Thought and Action* by S. I. Hayakawa.

Here I am concerned with a small but important section of Korzybski's ideas—in Hayakawa's phrase, 'the ladder of abstraction'. It was no new idea that all words are abstract but some are more abstract than others, but Korzybski worked out this idea very fully and devised a piece of apparatus for the purpose of training people in the appreciation of the different levels of abstraction at which they used words. He built his whole system of ideas round this and the messianic aspect referred to comes in with the fact that he believed his 'non-Aristotelian', as he called it, system had within it the potentiality of curing most, if not all, of the world's intellectual and emotional ills. It would be a pity if Korzybski's great enthusiasm for his system prevented a sympathetic examination of it by educationists; it will not cure even all the educational ills of the world but it helps to create an attitude towards language that is likely to lead to clearer thinking.

The accompanying diagram summarises the 'ladder of abstraction'.

The lowest level of all is what Korzybski calls the 'unspeakable level'. It is common knowledge nowadays that all matter consists of locked-up energy. The paper these words are printed on is, of course, paper, but it is also a mass of molecules that are themselves compounded of atoms that are themselves 'vibrant energy'. The paper then is a series of events in space-time. We are not aware of these events; not one of them is detectable. Their existence is known as a result of physicists and chemists working with a great variety of materials. Even the chemist who may be able to give the chemical formula for this paper cannot begin to take all these particular events into account; they are unrecordable, 'unspeakable'.

At the next level we come to the 'thing' as our senses tell us it is. This is a quite different world from the world of space-time events; it is the world of what we call real things. The paper is reasonably white, reasonably smooth and so on. It is what our senses tell us it is, and our senses are abstracting agents.

We next come to the label level of language. Hayakawa gives here a proper name, the name 'Bessie' applied to a particular cow. The name stands for a particular cow. There are, of course, many facts about Bessie that the name will not refer to in particular contexts. There is no mention in Hayakawa's brief synopsis of the 'ladder of abstraction' of the possibility that the name does not stand for the object but for a particular person's experience of the object. 'Bessie' indeed stands for the same cow to the farmer's wife who reared her from a calf and the butcher who buys the fully-grown cow; but the content of the name will be very different to these two people.

At the next level there is the word 'cow' meaning the class we call 'cow'. Here all the characteristics that mark Bessie or any other cow as individual are left out. We have abstracted, for the purpose of inclusion, the characteristic common to all cows.

Next we come to a more general term still 'livestock' where we include only those characteristics that Bessie has in common with other farm animals.

Hayakawa gives three more levels of abstraction exemplified successively by the terms 'farm assets', 'assets' and 'wealth'. Each of them may include Bessie, but more and more remotely. With 'wealth' the top rung of the ladder is reached in Hayakawa's example, but there is a type of word usage which ought to have its place on the ladder and is not given any place in Hayakawa's example. This is the usage in which the words appear to refer to the thing they name but do not in fact do so as in the sentence: 'What an ugly beast that cow is!' or 'What a magnificent animal that cow is!'

These appear to be statements about cows, but they are in fact statements about the person who is speaking. In the first of these statements, for example, he is saying: 'That cow produces in me the feeling I have whenever I see something that I call ugly.'

The kind of linguistic analysis which concentrates on the degrees of abstraction in language is likely to help students to develop insight not only into language but into the workings of their own minds. Techniques in this field applicable to the secondary school stage have still to be worked out, however, and at the primary stage of schooling the matter may perhaps be best left to the teacher who, if familiar with the basic theory and convinced of its usefulness, will find opportunities for bringing those ideas into her teaching in a simple way.

Over the page I give a summary diagram of the 'Ladder of Abstraction' as applied to the use of the word 'rose'—name of flower. The diagram is to be read from the bottom up:—

'a beautiful rose' (beauty)		The statement is not about the rose but about the speaker.
'national wealth' The rose-growing industry		Even the qualities that belong in all living things are left out. What remains is mere market value.
'living things' Still larger class		Even those qualities characteristic of all plants are left out.
'plants' Still larger class		Includes only those qualities which roses possess along with all plants.
'flower' Larger class		Includes the rose, but only in so far as it is analogous to all flowers.
'rose' Any rose		Qualities common to all roses included. The special individual qualities of the particular rose are left out.
'That rose', e.g. indicated by pointing		Includes everything it is possible to include about that rose, but much is necessarily left out.

Level of Sensory Perception.

The atomic level. Korzybski's 'unspeakable' level.

THE PRACTICAL ASPECT

These matters hardly concern the primary school pupil directly. Their application higher up the school seems self-evident.

Chapter 6

THE DYNAMICS
OF COMMUNICATION

THIS chapter deals with the process of communication in a fuller way than has so far been attempted in this book. The earlier chapters were concerned mainly with the relationships between 'things', names of 'things' and concepts. Here our concern is with what might be called the mental dynamics of communication, the mental forces that come into play during the processes of communication.

On earlier pages it was argued that since a word is not the 'thing' it stands for and since the meaning of a word to each of us as individuals is our experience of the 'thing' the word stands for, then we are never speaking directly about 'things' but only, and always, about our experiences of 'things'.

This idea has interesting implications when carried forward into a fuller consideration of what happens when we speak or write to one another.

The root implication from which all other implications spring is that *words do not carry meanings from one mind to another*.

It is possible that some readers of this book will find that statement surprising—at first glance, even incredible —because our conventional way of speaking and writing about these matters tends to make us assume that the essential fact about communication is precisely that words do carry meanings from one person to another.

'The meaning I really want to convey is . . .'

'For such feelings language by itself is an inadequate vehicle of expression . . .'

'Certainly his words carried their full cargo of meaning . . .'

'He put his ideas across with every appearance of absolute conviction . . .'

Behind each of these statements and many others like them lies the assumption that the speaker sends both words and meaning together across to his hearer who thereupon extracts the meaning. To say that anyone extracts meaning from words is, however, to speak figuratively. It may not be possible to escape metaphor entirely in speaking about this process, but a more literal description of what happens is that, far from extracting a speaker or writer's meaning from his words, we put *our* meanings into them. Meanings could be *extracted* only if they came across with the words and this is not the case.

Certainly, when someone speaks and we understand him it is *as though* the meaning has come across with the words, but it is only *as though*. What has happened in such a case is that the hearer put into the speaker's words the meaning that the speaker intended him to put.

The following diagram and comment on it may help to make this clearer.

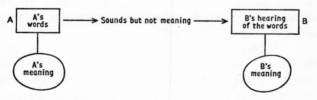

A has something to tell B. That something is connected with an experience or experiences. He chooses words to fit the experience. He sends those words across to B in the form of sound-waves. Those sound-waves—and they alone—reach B. B, however, has already in his past experience learned to associate those particular sound-patterns with particular percepts or concepts and it is these, from *his* own experience, that come to his mind on hearing A's words. When the experiences of A and B are sufficiently alike, it *seems* as though the meaning has come across with the sounds. But it is only *as though*. To believe that it actually does is to fall into one of the commonest delusions that perplex the mind of man. The language-habits that imply that meanings are transferred from one mind to another by means of language no doubt originated in this confusion of *as though* with *fact*. Certainly those language habits of which I have given a few examples do a great deal to buttress the delusion. An interesting example of how deeply founded is the delusion is the use of the phrase 'reading into'. Normally this phrase is used to express the idea that someone is not taking the right meaning out of the words. And yet, as we have seen, there is no possibility of taking the right or wrong meaning out of words but only of putting meanings, right or wrong, into them. We must *always* 'read into'.

It would seem to follow from these statements that nobody ever learned anything from discussion or reading. For if a man merely puts meanings into words, what can he be learning from the words? And where do the meanings come from in the first instance?

In Chapters 2 and 3 the beginnings of language in the young human being were discussed. There we saw that the giving of one name to things that were in appearance different resulted in a re-ordering of the child's perceptual experiences. The primrose is very different from the rose but because they are both called 'flower', they are conceived as being similar. There is at the same time a contrary process at work. In learning to speak, the child is also learning that some things that are alike are not quite so closely alike as they seem. The 'thing' in the field is not to be called 'goggie' (doggie) even though it looks as though it ought to have that name; it is to be called 'sheep'. Thus through the classifying of experiences meanings are acquired. Each new meaning thus acquired leads to the acquisition of further meanings. During childhood new experiences are continually crowding into the developing mind and with them new meanings. In adult life the completely new experience is rare. One may travel in some foreign country for the first time and see many things one has not seen before, but the experiences that come during these travels are not lived through in an intrinsic newness but are always seen or felt against the background of previous experience, even against the background of what we have imagined the experiences were going to be. Our imaginings are themselves built upon direct experiences. We choose, shall we say, to holiday in a particular country because we have heard that there we shall get really hot weather—a warmer sun than we have ever known before. Though we may not have known the sun so hot before, we nevertheless have a good idea of what to expect: since we have known it hot, we can imagine it hotter. The reality indeed may exceed our imaginings, but our imaginings are there to exceed, to fit, or to be exceeded.

These experience-based meanings are the meanings we put into the words we hear or read. An experience may have a new quality about it, yet the mind immediately sets about assimilating the new to the old. If through word of mouth or print we learn something new, it is either because the words have drawn our attention to something we have not noticed before or because we have had to re-pattern our past experiences in order to put the appropriate meanings into the words we have heard or read.

While I was working on this chapter, for example, I

learned a set of facts that were quite new to me and that I
would never have imagined. Are they facts? I have only a
newspaper report to go on, but most of the 'facts' I accept
are similarly second-hand. The newspaper report contained the astonishing statement that astronauts in orbit
have been able to detect objects as small as lorries, lamp-
posts and factory chimneys from a distance of a hundred
miles. I find this astonishing because my past experience
of seeing things at a distance leads me to think that it is
impossible for the naked eye to see with that degree of
definition from the distance my past experience tells me
a hundred miles is. Another set of items from my previous
knowledge makes that piece of information still more
astonishing; it is the set of facts that I have picked up
about the way in which the eye works. There did not seem
to be any loop-hole for the entry of a statement about such
detailed perception from so great a distance. And yet,
though the report did not explain the whole process to me,
it did suggest a direction in which the explanation might
lie in terms on to which I could fit a meaning: in normal
situations the eye is in a constant state of vibration and in
the state of weightlessness the rate of vibration greatly
increases. My past experience is such as to allow me to fit
at least a vague meaning on to the term vibration even
though the report does not state what sort of vibration is
being referred to—and so, if I were able to pursue the subject, the way lies open for me to acquire still more new
facts about the nature of visual perception.

Not all the new ideas that come to us do so so directly
as a result of words that someone else uses in speech or
print. The idea underlying this chapter, for example, that
words do not carry meanings across from one mind to
another, was some time ago a new one to me. Yet nobody
ever told me things were so; the idea emerged as a result

of the coming together of two sets of ideas that I had long been familiar with. Since those ideas are closely concerned with linguistic communication it will be appropriate to describe here how the re-alignment of ideas took place.

For many years I had been interested in communication. For as many years I had accepted without question the pattern of thought suggested by 'what I mean to convey' and similar expressions implying that the communicator was sending across meanings as well as sounds. On the day when, as it seemed to me I became able to cast aside the metaphor and look at the process clearly, I had been becoming increasingly impatient with the treatment of language common in behaviourist text-books, that of regarding words as stimuli to which people reacted like complicated animals – no more. Where was consciousness of self? Where were 'self-reverence, self-knowledge, self-control' in the mechanistic stimulus-response world described in so many of those books? At the same time— and here was the converging line of thought—I was trying to sort out in my mind the 'things' (in this case 'processes') which one might legitimately associate with the words 'sign', 'signal' and 'symbol'. In one of those text-books I found the words 'signal' and 'stimulus' treated as though they were synonymous.

I found myself thinking of radio-signals passing at the speed of light into outer space and setting in motion series of events in inter-planetary missiles and began to wonder in what respect signals controlling the firing mechanisms of guide-rockets in space could be compared to, or differentiated from, that other type of signal we call words. I wondered, too, in what respect radio-signals of that kind could be compared with the stimuli of the behaviourists. The more I thought of these things, the more clearly the differences between types of signal emerged and nothing stood out more clearly than the fact that the signals controlling the direction of the inter-planetary missile had no more connection with linguistic communication than a ship has with a fish. The apparatus at the control centre and the apparatus in the missile itself were both parts of a system just as a bell-push is part of a system which includes the bell. The fact that millions of miles might intervene between the parts of the system, however greatly it might increase the technical difficulties, did not alter the nature of the case. The radio-waves were no more a signal to the appropriate parts of the missile than the push on a bell-push is a signal to the bell. They were no more a set of stimuli to these parts than the turning of the steering-wheel is a signal to the wheels of a car—change in one part of the system caused change, on rigidly designed lines, in another part of the system. When one end of a see-saw moves, the other end moves too. You could no more say that meanings were sent out to the missile than you could that meaning travels from one end of the see-saw to the other.

I began thinking about the signals that result in the television pictures on our screens. These were obviously, in one sense at least, different from the radio-signals of sound radio even though in one sense they were the same. At first thought it seemed that television was a case in which signals actually carried the message. Was the message not the picture televised and did not that come across as a series of analogues. A moment's reflection showed, however, that the television waves no more carried meanings than did the radio-waves of sound radio.

Normally in thinking of television one associates it with two types of signal—and this is in one sense accurate: there are signals which carry the analogues of the sounds picked up by the microphone and others that carry analogues of what the camera cells have picked up. The student of 'communication', however, will readily see that there are three types of signal in any television broadcast:

A: Signals that carry analogues of the scene televised, e.g. a show-jumping competition.

B. Signals that carry the analogues of the sounds that are a natural part of the scene televised, e.g. the sound of the horses' hoofs.

C. Signals which carry the analogues of the sounds spoken by the commentator.

At first I rushed to the conclusion that signals A and B carried the meanings to which the commentator had put the words represented by the C signals. This implied, however, that words were labels directly applied to things, a view that I had earlier rejected in favour of what seemed the more accurate one that the meanings of words were not the things themselves but our experiences of the things.

The next stage in unlocking this Chinese puzzle was to wonder whether it would not be more fitting to describe the situation in the following terms:

The A and B signals stand for the events out of which the commentator gets his meanings and the C signals represent the words into which the viewer/listener puts *his* meanings.

Even when formulating that sentence, however, I saw that it was grossly over-simplified since it ignored the previous experience of both commentator and viewer. It also ignored that commentator's *intention* which would largely determine his choice of the 'things' inside the general picture that needed to be spoken about as well as determining his choice of words in speaking about them. The meanings did indeed lie in the previous experience of both commentator and viewer; the A and B signals merely contained representations of the events from which the meanings in the light of past experience were extracted and upon which, also in the light of past experience, meanings were imposed.

The process of thinking round these things at the same time showed how inadequate the behaviourist stimulus-response view of language was. A dog responds to the word 'biscuit'—yes; and that word in that context can undoubtedly be regarded as of the same order as the bell which Pavlov set ringing with such persistence in the corridors of psychology, but how different are the events in the human mind.

On an earlier page there was given an instance of the tumult of associations that can come into a human mind, each association setting off other associations in a way that cannot possibly happen with any of the lower animals. The reactions of human beings are so very much more complicated than any in the sub-human world can possibly be that the bell/saliva analogy has no sure validity. Human beings in the early years of life may certainly be said to respond to stimuli very much as animals do, but with the acquisition of language and of consciousness of self the human being enters a new dimension. Brain becomes mind, one might say; for linguistic activity and consciousness of self are the chief characteristics of 'mind'.

True, in a great many of the language transactions of everyday life adult human beings do respond to words in a simple stimulus-response way—as when a husband, without lifting his eyes from the paper he is reading, passes his wife the salt in response to her request. Matters are very different, however, when communication that requires numerous and near-simultaneous references to past experience is concerned. Here the interpretation of words can almost be said to become a series of creative acts. The speaker or writer is selecting items from past and present experience and selecting the words to go with them; the listener or reader on his part is doing a similar thing; his references may begin with present, immediate experience but at the same time he is referring to his past experience, even re-ordering or re-patterning it, in such a way as to be able to put into the words he has heard or read the meanings the speaker or reader intends him to put. These meanings are not of the intellect only, of course; the emotions are also heavily involved and just as frequently.

There is a great range of level at which this activity may take place. The particular level on any occasion will depend greatly upon the purpose of the communication and upon the quality of mind of the people concerned. There are people whose communications seldom appear to rise much above the level of 'pass the salt' or 'switch on the television'. On the other hand there are people whose communications make a heavy demand upon the creative power of the listener or reader. In many cases the exercise of that creative power results in new insights and it is in the processes leading to those new insights that the vast difference between animal and human activity is most clearly marked.

Behind every act of communication there is some purpose. The purpose may be trivial or serious; it may be deliberate or unconscious, overt or hidden. A speaker may honestly believe that the purpose of his communication is 'this' while his hearer deduces that the purpose is 'that' — and in some cases the hearer may be right. Whatever the purpose may be in any particular case, that purpose affects the form of the communication; and similarly the purpose in the listener's mind affects the meanings he will put into the words he hears. Any normal act of communication that rises above the simple stimulus-response level involves complicated processes and my intention in the second half of this chapter is to build up a diagrammatic representation of the main processes.

There is a perfectly understandable objection to the use of diagrams to illustrate some linguistic processes. I have seen graphs, for example, that were intended to show the rise and fall of intensity of emotion in a poem. Such a use of diagrams seems singularly inept. If the reader of a poem is unable to read into the words themselves the emotional rhythm, then the graph will mean nothing to him. On the other hand, if he is able to do so, then the graph is unnecessary and perhaps worse than unnecessary since it is likely to bring in associations that have nothing to do with the poem at all. Diagrammatic representation has, however, been found very useful in clarifying descriptions of complicated processes. For example, in trying to map out various functions of the brain, neurologists have found block diagrams very useful. A block diagram is more abstract—more general—than a blueprint; it omits the detail inside particular units but shows the relationship between units. The next few pages will attempt to build up a diagram illustrating the processes of communication in the belief that as a result of so doing some clarification will be achieved.

We start then with a set of real events, the 'thing' the communication is about. This 'thing' may be a simple object like a pencil which, though it is indeed the resultant of a vast number of space-time events at the atomic level, is neverthless a simple object as perceived by our senses; or it may be a complicated series of events like a drawing by Rembrandt or a series of events of a different kind like Magna Carta or the Declaration of Independence. Whatever they are these events have, or had, an existence outside the minds of the people speaking about them. This 'thing' referred to, this referent, I shall represent by a plain circle.

The circle will not be used for any of the other concepts involved in the process of communication; the 'thing itself' stands apart from everything else, apart even from our concept of it. Some modern philosophers dismiss the idea of the 'thing in itself' as being an old-fashioned concept, but I cannot see how in speaking about communication this idea can be done away with. The tree standing outside my window is different from my idea of it. We need therefore a symbol to represent a person's concept of the 'thing'. For this I shall use a crescent shape. The simple diagram given below, therefore, represents a 'thing in itself' and two concepts of it—that of the person who is speaking and that of the person who is listening. It will be noted that the symbols of the concepts of the 'thing' are not regular crescents nor are they identical. The differences in the symbols indicate that the two people do not have the same concepts of the 'thing'.

It is necessary, too, to have a symbol indicating purpose, for the purposes of both speaker and listener affect both the manner and the matter of the communication. For this I shall use triangles. The triangle indicating the speaker's purpose will naturally be different from the one indicating the purpose of the person he is speaking to, for even if the purposes are ostensibly the same there will inevitably be some differences. The double-headed arrows linking purposes to concepts show that the purposes influence the concept and vice versa. At the same time they also point to the fact that the concept one has of anything is not a fixed unalterable but changes with the context which includes the purpose:

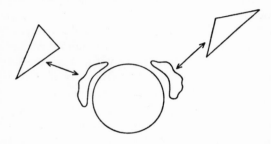

It is also necessary to have in our diagram a symbol representing meaning. It would simplify matters if 'concept' and 'meaning' were identical, but this is not so. Concepts are necessarily involved in meaningful statements, but in any act of communication we are not referring to our concepts about various things but are making statements about them and this implies a bringing together of different concepts into possibly new combinations. Meaning, then, will be represented by irregularly curved shapes:

For the sake of clarity I shall now give only the speaker's side of the picture. The hearer's side will be given in the completed diagram:

Another necessary factor is past experience. That is, of course, implied in both concept and meaning, but it is so

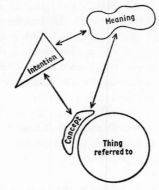

important a factor that the diagram would be lacking in proper emphasis if it were not included. Past experience will be represented by an irregular quadrilateral figure. Here again arrows indicate interaction between the elements:

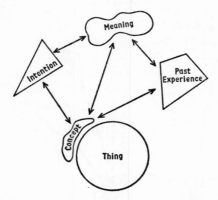

One thing ought to be stressed particularly. It is that in both purpose and past experience emotion plays a strong part. I have not chosen a separate symbol to represent emotional forces because they permeate the whole process of communication equally with the intellectual.

Finally we have the symbols by which communication is affected, in this case the spoken words, the sounds that pass from one person to another into which the speaker has put his meaning and into which, he hopes, his listener will put a meaning not too radically different from his own. The language is symbolised by a rectangle. Here, too, the arrows show the influences that bear upon the choice of words and their arrangement in connected speech. The full diagram appears below and is followed by further explanatory comment.

This diagram still omits many details but to include more would complicate matters more than it would clarify them. The most important factor that is omitted is prob-

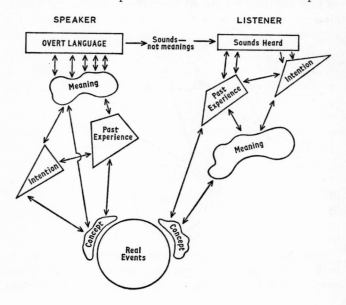

ably inner speech. The diagram shows 'overt language' to indicate with as little complication as possible the fact that the words that are spoken are not the only linguistic events that take place, for as one speaks there is a continual selection of terms going on, implying at the same time a rejection of terms that have come into consciousness. Another important factor that is not shown is the influence in spoken communication of non-linguistic signs such as facial expression and tone of voice.

The series of arrows between meaning and overt language on the speaker's side of the diagram indicates that there is a continuing interaction between meaning and the words spoken. We sometimes find, for example, that when we have said something the meaning becomes clearer to ourselves.

This diagram will have fuller meaning if seen against the earlier and simpler diagrams illustrating the process of linguistic communication which showed the presence of intrusive associations as this skeleton diagram does not. The presence of these other associations is suggested by the use of 'overt' for these associations are bound up with inner speech. 'Overt language' is language selected and ordered for the purposes of communication within the framework that custom decrees is suitable for public utterance—even though the 'public' consists of only one other person. That overt language emerges out of an underlying private language, a language which during the process of communication is continually being interrupted by the necessity for giving the words an expected order and form. When these interruptions do not take place the private language takes that form to which Joyce gave artistic representation in *Ulysses* and *Finnegan's Wake*.

It will be noted that the elements on the two sides of the diagram are differently ordered. The listener will normally have a different starting-point. He may not even at the out-set have a purpose in listening; the purpose may be created by what he hears. As soon as he has that purpose, however, he immediately becomes involved in the process of putting meanings into the sounds he hears by reference to past experience and present context.

In this process of communication everything has a certain degree of fluidity. True, words have the same meanings more or less from day to day and from context to context — but it is only *more or less*. Even 'things in themselves' may be changed as a result of communication: the great influence of scientific research upon our environment is witness to that fact. And we ourselves are continually changing as a result of the impact of linguistic communication. Past events in themselves, of course, do not change, but our concepts of the past, whether of our own past or of anything past are continually subject to change. We never step into the same river twice.

I have mentioned the fact that non-linguistic symbols might have been included in the diagram. The reason for their omission is entirely because the complication of diagrams defeats their very purpose. These non-linguistic symbols are, however, extremely important in communication and call for further comment.

As we shall see linguistic and non-linguistic symbols are not always sharply distinguishable. Moreover, some are intentional and some are not. Some originate in the mind of the communicator; some are part of a context designed by a third party who is not present and has no interest in the details of any particular communication that is taking place.

The bank manager does not go to his office in working hours wearing the clothes he uses for working in the garden on Saturday afternoon. His moderately formal clothes are non-linguistic symbols by means of which he tells his customer that his money is safe in the bank or that the bank is substantial enough to lend him money. His office itself, designed by others for his use and the use of his successor, is such as to give whatever words are spoken in it the authority of material stability and complete reliability. Some American banks were so successful in doing so that they had to launch a campaign designed to let people know that the banks were not as formal as they appeared. An architect when he is planning a building is not indulging in self-expression, though he tries to work in some of that, he is for a large part of the time designing non-linguistic symbols that will be part of the context in which linguistic communication is carried on. This is true of banks, cathedrals, company offices and often private houses. The ritual of church services is itself a series of largely non-linguistic symbols that operate in an environment designed to give solemnity to the words spoken. A recent report claimed that one way of getting a somewhat better price for a house was to get a friend to park a sleek sports car in front of it regularly enough to give the impression that the people who lived there had a certain 'class'—another non-linguist symbol. The hostess who has her hair done before guests arrive and who sees that everything is tidy in the house and that the flowers are properly arranged in the vases is by means of non-linguistic symbols setting the tone in which conversation will take place. So too the young lover with his oiled hair, the pop-singer with his special hair-cut, and the girl with the slit skirt and stiletto heels. Vast industries have grown up for no other reason than to produce non-linguistic symbols which will influence the meanings put into the linguistic ones. Their production is a main concern of the advertising industry, the cosmetics industry, of the packaging industry. Artists, architect designers of every description, photographers, lithographers, chemists, printers, silversmiths, hairdressers, dentists, plastic surgeons—there is no end to the list of people whose lives are devoted to the business of creating contexts which will induce people to put a particular meaning into the words that are sent their way.

Here we come to a point at which the word 'symbol' itself becomes difficult. In an earlier note I referred to the difficulty caused by the lack of precise definition in the uses of the terms 'sign' and 'symbol'. Now there comes the question as to whether something that has the same kind of effect as a symbol but which is neither audible, visible nor tangible, which may not even be intentional can yet be classed as a symbol. I have in mind a pause in the course of speech. Such a pause—as in an actor's timing—is sheer absence of sound. Yet it has significance coming from the words that preceded it and those that are expected to come after it. It is also deliberate and in any case speech is as full of pauses as of words. The question as to whether a pause is to be regarded as a symbol, linguistic or non-linguistic, whether it is intentional or not, is of minor importance. It is important, however, that if we decide that this cannot be classed as a symbol, we ought not to let that decision blind us to the fact that a pause may have the same kind of effect as those 'things' that we have regarded as symbols, linguistic and non-linguistic both. Furthermore the pause I am speaking of falls into the class of tone of voice and tone of voice is in effect not easily separated from the smile or the frown which are definitely non-linguistic. Accent and pronunciation, too, have this kind of significance. The same words spoken at a trades union conference, first in a public school accent and then in a voice with the accent of the factory floor will not have the same meanings put into them by the audience—and that does not so drastically outrage logic since it is unlikely that two speakers coming to the same words by such different routes would themselves have completely agreed as to what they meant. The structure of sentences belongs to the same category. A spoken sentence that is very well turned will to one person suggest that he is someone who has really mastered the problem he is discussing and to another that he is someone so glib that he cannot be speaking spontaneously from the heart.

These side-elements have on the whole the greatest force and liveliness in relation to the spoken word although the use, for example, of sex-symbols is endemic in advertising copy. The printed word has nevertheless some help —or hindrance—from these intrusive influences. A poem is helped by its placing on the printed page; a perfectly good book may be passed over on the library shelf because it is badly printed and if it is taken out the reader may find he has a prejudice to work against when reading it on that same account. And a simple statement of the obvious by a well-known name may be seen to be a revealed truth whereas the same thing written by a nonentity will be passed over as the kind of thing one would expect a nonentity to write.

THE PRACTICAL ASPECT

Nearly the whole of this chapter refers to a level of linguistic experience beyond that of children in the primary school. If children start thinking about communication they may stop communicating! Among the important non-linguistic symbols used in communication, however, are those of mime and dramatic performance—gesture, movement, stage-settings. There are few teachers in primary schools nowadays who have not some experience of class-room drama as well as the 'school play'. The content of this chapter gives no suggestions about the use of class-room drama, but it does perhaps give a convincing argument in favour of linking the non-linguistic symbols to the linguistic ones. A lesson in language can be a lesson in communication without words. Get a child to tell the class something without using words and you are preparing the ground for later insight into the processes of communication. The connection between expression through music and movement is obvious.

Similarly the non-linguistic symbols ought to be used along with the written symbols in the pupils' written work. The *appearance* of an exercise book says something. If a pupil knows that, he is likely to take greater care.

Perhaps even more important is the fact that 'good manners' is nothing but a series of largely non-linguistic symbols creating a context in which the linguistic symbols can work freely. In other words the 'well-mannered' person, you might say, is one with whom conversation is easy. I put 'well-mannered' in inverted commas because its meaning varies. The same difficulty faces the teacher here as when she attempts to give children a form of speech that conflicts with the home background.

As for the secondary stage, it seems to me that the content of this chapter, suitably simplified, can form a frame of reference for many language lessons and could form the basis of a series of lessons.

Chapter 7

THE LANGUAGE OF
MATHEMATICS

IF a revolution can be said to be taking place in any part of the educational field now, it is in the teaching of mathematics. In many parts of the country experiments are going on with methods and materials based upon ideas that had not reached the training colleges, or departments of education, at the time when most of the teachers now in schools were in training. These ideas are furthermore couched in a language that is at present foreign to many teachers, though there are increased numbers who are taking an interest in the new ideas.

That the term 'mathematics' should be used of anything that is taught at the primary stage is in itself a mildly revolutionary idea because traditionally the primary schools have devoted themselves to that branch of mathematics which goes by the name of arithmetic and to somewhat narrow aspects even of that. Now there are primary schools in which mathematical ideas are being explored that most grammar schools do not yet regard as being within their province.

Since this book is concerned with language in education, the story of how this development came about is only marginally within its compass. Here it will be enough to say that there appear to be three main reasons for these changes: 1. the general and continuing reaction against rote learning of the nineteenth century type; 2. changes in mathematical thinking itself; 3, the impact of technology.

It may well be thought that there is little place for a chapter on mathematics in a book concerned with language. After all, the specifically mathematical statements in a mathematical text-book are not printed in ordinary 'words' at all, and in many books dealing with advanced mathematics ordinary printed words play a very small part. Moreover, the symbols of mathematics at the more advanced levels are quite incomprehensible to people who can read with understanding books of most other kinds. Clearly there is something very special about the printed symbols of mathematics, so special perhaps that it is not accurate to treat them as part of language.

Fortunately the discussion of the nature of mathematical language does not require the specialist knowledge necessary for the understanding of the symbols of advanced mathematics any more than the ability to 'hear in the mind' is necessary for the understanding of the nature of a musical score. Fortunately, too, such a discussion does throw some light, dispersed though it may be, upon the nature of mathematical thinking.

The print on this page, as I have pointed out earlier, is not language; it does not in the strict sense consist of words but of symbols that stand for words that in their turn stand for percepts, concepts, or feelings. So when we write 'three' we have set down the name of a particular concept by means of a set of conventional symbols, in this case symbols tied to the sounds that make up that name in the English language. When we write '3' we have set down the name of that same concept by means of another kind of symbol. The numeral '3' is therefore no more and no less a word than is 'three'. The numeral '3' is tied to the whole word 'three' in precisely the same way as the digraph 'th' is tied to the initial sound of the spoken word 'three'—that is, by convention.

There are two main differences between 3 and 'three':
(*a*) the numeral is a single symbol, (*b*) it is not tied to the
sounds of any particular language.

The fact that the basic numerals are single symbols is
important; the use of columns for recording higher values
would not be possible otherwise and, besides, the ease
with which the ten uncomplicated symbols of our counting system can be visualised lies behind our powers of
mental calculation.

The fact that these number-symbols are not tied to the
separate sounds of words has given rise to an idea that one
frequently encounters in books on elementary arithmetic —
namely, that the numerals represent ideas, not words.
There is a confusion of thought here. True, both the
Russian child and the English child understand the same
numerals, but the Russian child interprets them through
the medium of the Russian words just as the English
child does so through the English words. The numerals,
therefore, are a printed form of language: $3+2=5$ is as
much a sentence as 'The quick brown fox jumped over the
lazy dog'. It is not a metaphorical use of the word 'language', therefore, to speak of 'the language of arithmetic',
nor, since mathematics is an extension of arithmetic, to
speak of 'the language of mathematics'.

From the simple language of numbers that everyone is
familiar with we can deduce some significant facts about
the nature of mathematical language.

The first of these is that the language of mathematics is
a logical structure that is consistent within itself. A mathematician might qualify this statement, pointing to a number of paradoxes that have troubled mathematicians for
centuries, but even so he is likely to agree that, at the level
of mathematics likely to be encountered in any school,
logical consistency is an essential characteristic. He might

even go further and say that generally even he himself treats the paradoxes as non-existent.

A second fact that emerges is that the language of mathematics does not have the same kind of relationship to real things as ordinary non-mathematical language. We have seen in our earlier discussion that the meanings of the symbols of ordinary language lie in their association (through experience) with things in the non-symbolic world. Ordinary language is in general meaningful only when it directs the attention to experiences that are in the form of percepts of real things or concepts or feelings that have arisen out of experiences of real things. This is not true in quite the same way of the language of mathematics.

It will probably be fairly generally agreed that the concept of number arises out of the perception of the differences between small quantities. The most primitive languages have an extremely limited number vocabulary. Indeed it is maintained by anthropologists that some primitive languages had no more than three words of a specifically numerical kind—a word for 'one', a word for 'two', and a word for 'three'. Any quantity greater than three was designated by a word equivalent to our 'many'. Children when they learn to count must also begin with those small numbers. The reason lies in the nature of human perception. The human eye and brain are not so constituted as to be able to distinguish between the quantities in a random group of, say, nine and a group of ten with the same sort of immediacy as it can distinguish between, say, a spoon and a fork, but even a child of pre-school age can learn to distinguish between a group of two and a group of three. Practice will no doubt enable older people to distinguish in that immediate way between somewhat larger groups— but not very much larger. The group of nine, if it is randomly distributed, can never be seen instantly as not being a group of eight or ten. One can confidently say that there are nine objects in the group only by running up a number-scale of words on the basis of a one-to-one relationship between the separate objects in the group and the number-words. It will be evident from these statements that the whole number-system is a vast structure of inter-related symbols based upon very limited percepts. It is like a vast inverted pyramid poised upon its apex, the apex representing the contact with the world of ordinary perception: perception of the difference between one object and no object, one object and two objects, two objects and three objects . . . and many objects. At the other end of the scale is the idea of infinity which is not connected with the world of ordinary perception at all but is a logical derivative of the scale that began with these primitive percepts. Similar logical extensions result in such concepts as those represented by $0/0$ and $\sqrt{-1}$ which, though they may be traced back to those primitive perceptions of differences between small quantities, have no other basis in reality whatsoever. So it can be said that apart from its very slight contact with the world of ordinary perception—so slight and so distant that it can easily be thought not to exist at all—the mathematics of number exists as a complicated mental structure independent of real things. If it is true that the whole of mathematics is an extension of arithmetic, as some of the great mathematicians have held, then this independence of reality extends to the whole of mathematics. Russell and Whitehead maintained that the whole of mathematics could be established on the basis of logical principles alone. Yet it seems to me that logic must have percepts to work with and I have indicated what seem to me the minimum number of percepts necessary for establishing the mathematics of number. All the familiar aspects of arithmetic follow rather easily from these percepts. The concept of matching one-to-one with objects on one side and words on the other quickly leads to the idea of an unending series; the concept of positive numbers has an easy analogy in the concept of an infinite series of negative numbers; the idea of writing the numbers down in columns has another easy analogy in the writing of fractions in columns —decimal fractions. All thinking is based on analogy I said on an earlier page. Nowhere is this more evident than in the evolution of arithmetical ideas.

The 'unreality' of mathematics may not be thought to have much connection with mathematics in the primary school where one of the major trends is to make use of the environment in order to make mathematics real to the learning child and where it is equally the intention to use mathematics in order to lead the child towards the discovery of aspects of reality that would otherwise remain hidden from him. And yet it is well for the teacher to realise, however vaguely, that mathematically speaking the 'real' experiences the child has in this connection are in the end valuable only in so far as they lead him to appreciate the 'unreal' world of mathematical relationships.

During the past century or so there has been a coming together of two subjects that were formerly regarded as separate—mathematics and logic. Since this is a book for teachers, it will not be out of place at this point to mention the work of the one-time struggling headmaster of a small private school in Lincoln, George Boole. In what time he could find while still running his school, Boole devoted his considerable mental energies to the study of his two main interests—mathematics and logic. His work in these fields was so successful that he was given the opportunity of following a university course. In this he was successful to the extent of becoming professor of mathematics in Dublin. Boole wrote a number of books in both mathematics and logic. He called one of them *The Laws of Thought*. In some of his work in logic Boole used mathematical symbols and here we have an early sign of the *rapprochement* of mathematics and logic which is characteristic of today. One of the major works in mathematics of the twentieth century is *Principia Mathematica* by Whitehead and Russell who, as already indicated, wrote from the standpoint that mathematics is a branch of logic. In an essay on 'Mathematical Logic' Russell refers to the phrase 'laws of thought' as 'quaint', but no one was ever more interested in the concepts that most people would expect to be associated with that phrase, and, somewhat belatedly, it is these concepts in a very elementary form that are giving school mathematics a new form today.

What is so very new about the newest developments in primary school mathematics is that an outright attempt is being made to lead children on to an appreciation of the logical aspects of mathematics using language of a kind that until recently had never appeared in a school book at any level. If any reader has any doubt about this, let him look at the *Bulletins* of the Nuffield Mathematics Project. In *Bulletin No. 2* he will find the following exercise:

Which of the following sentences show the symmetric property? (Note; The meaning of 'the symmetric property' has previously been explained by examples.)

> Jack lives in the same road as John.
> 4×3 is a smaller number than 4×4.
> Doris is taller than Joan.
> The green box fits inside the red box.

In *Bulletin No. 3* he will find diagrams such as these, with explanatory comments, in a discussion of 'mapping'.

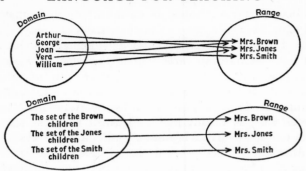

This instance is of the conversion of many:one mapping to one:one mapping.

These *Bulletins*, it is necessary to point out, are intended as forum for discussion for teachers but they do contain suggestions in some detail for actual class-room lessons even though the main work of presentation for school use is in process of separate publication in experimental form. I have given those glimpses of the ideas as an indication of the direction the workers in the Nuffield Project hope the teaching of mathematics at the primary stage will take.

The Nuffield Mathematics Teaching Project came into being on September 1st, 1964, and there is undoubtedly a great deal of work to be done before the ideas set out in the *Bulletins* are in a form that the teacher with little mathematical background can use with profit. The work will be to a very large extent a matter of finding the appropriate language. The object of the Teaching Project, as expressed by Dr Geoffrey Matthews, the organiser, is 'to produce a contemporary course for children from 5 to 13. This will be designed to help them to connect together many aspects of the world around them, to introduce them gradually to the processes of abstract thinking, and to foster in them a critical, logical, but also creative turn of mind.'

He goes on:

A synthesis will be made of what is worth preserving in the traditional work with various new ideas some of which are already being tried out . . . A concrete approach will be made to abstract concepts, and the children will make their own discoveries whenever possible. The work of the project will be set against the background of new thinking concerning mathematics itself . . . Any topic or aspect of the subject introduced must be more intelligible and purposeful (and so easier to teach) than what it replaces. Perhaps the most important message of 'modern' mathematics at this level is its ubiquity, the fact that doing sums is only a fraction of the programme envisaged.

And again: 'Almost everyone is anxious to break loose from the fossilised tyranny of Victorian arithmetic—the alternative is dynamic, flexible, vital mathematics.'

Sentiments of that kind have been very frequently expressed in recent years. So there is nothing new about *them*. In any case specific proposals are more important than well-meaning intentions. The revolutionary proposal of the Nuffield team, perhaps it would be more accurate to say of some of the Nuffield team, is to introduce 'the language of sets' into primary school mathematics for the reason that 'the whole of mathematics, no matter how complicated, can be expressed in the language and operations of sets so that much of mathematics can be made clearer, more precise and more of a unified whole by using the language of sets wherever it is convenient'.

Since the majority of teachers now in primary schools have not yet heard of the language of sets, it will be some time before the ideas of the Nuffield panel make a substantial impact upon the school. A new generation of teachers who have themselves some insight into the meaning and purpose of 'set theory' may have to come into the schools from the training colleges before primary mathematics takes this significant turn.

'I had never heard of "sets" before, nor for that matter of Venn diagrams,' wrote a teacher, who is himself a member of the Editorial Advisory Panel of the Nuffield Project, after reading *Bulletin No. 1*. 'I now know a little more about sets, but I still have to find out about Venn diagrams. I was so depressed at my lack of knowledge that I attempted to salvage my self-respect by a survey of my colleagues. Result? Not one of them had any idea about sets and none had heard of Venn diagrams.'

Lack of special knowledge is not the only obstacle to progress on the lines envisaged. Another obstacle lies in the difficulty of giving to the formalised logic of the language of sets a quality that will have some appeal to teachers who for several decades now had been encouraged to regard anything to which the word 'formal' could reasonably be applied as being against the spirit of true child education.

There can be no question of the truth of the claim that the language of sets is fundamental in mathematics today. There is a question, however, as to whether children at the primary stage can not only learn the symbols but grasp the concepts. The answer must wait until more work is done. The theory of language set out in this book does, however, suggest certain conditions that must be fulfilled if pupils are to gain insight into mathematics whether old or new.

The first condition is that the pupils must be given a sufficient number of sensory experiences to which the language they are learning may be attached, for in spite of the 'unreality' of mathematics, sensory experience of real things is the basis from which abstract concepts spring. A second is that the pupil must learn for himself, must acquire the meanings for himself. This follows because the language of mathematics, whether in 'set' terms or not, shares that characteristic of language in general emphasised in the chapter called 'The Dynamics of Communication' — namely that the meaning does not come across in the words and symbols but only appears to do so. The pupils must discover meanings for himself. Much is written nowadays about the role of discovery in learning, and the Nuffield *Bulletins* are not silent about this factor. The role of discovery is, however, usually referred to as though its educational value were chiefly motivational. The motivational element is indeed important, for discovery is a token of success and nothing more surely leads to further success, but the other aspect of 'discovery' brings us back again to our language theory. It implies that unless the pupil discovers the meanings for himself he has no meanings at all.

I have devoted a fair amount of space in this chapter to the suggestions of the Nuffield team not only because they are the most radical in this field but also because they are linguistic to an extent that no other suggested changes are. Meanwhile arithmetic in various guises predominates in primary schools. There are some linguistic aspects of this narrower subject to which I feel some attention needs to be drawn.

1. The numeral is not the number. This fact has been implied several times on previous pages. The practical importance of realising this fact cannot readily be pinpointed. A child will not be a better calculator for being aware of it, but his mathematical thinking is likely to be more truly orientated because of that awareness. For example, the child who realises that our way of writing down numbers is just one of many conventional ways will find it less difficult than one who has not that realisation to accept the notion that numbers can be written down in bases other than ten.

2. It would not be difficult to fill pages with quotations showing that many books written for use in schools do more to conceal than to reveal to children the nature of number. It is often assumed that because a child can count he knows what counting is. At what stage a child should be taught to think about the nature of counting it is difficult to say. Experiment may give an answer. Certainly it is not good that a student should emerge from a training college without ever having had to ask himself pertinent questions about what he is doing when he is counting and how number-words come to have the meanings we ascribe to them. I have found that the following simple ideas about numbers come as a surprise to many teachers:

The meaning of 6 is not : : : or any other arrangement of dots or anything else; the meaning of 6 is 'one more than 5'; the meaning of 5 is 'one more than 4' . . . and so on, and those meanings originate in our perceptual awareness of the differences between the smallest groups that there are. Further, the meaning of each of the number-words derives from the fact that they are spoken in a particular order as we run up the number scale; 6 has the meaning of 'one more than 5' because in the process of counting it is the word spoken immediately after 5.

It is possible to find which is the bigger of two groups without counting the items in the groups if these groups are of objects which we can move about as we wish, for then the objects can be matched one to one. If, for example, it is pennies we are dealing with, they can be put in two piles and the relative sizes of the piles will tell which is the bigger since, unless they are very much worn, pennies are all the same thickness; or objects can be spaced one-to-one along parallel lines and the longer line will indicate the larger group. This system could even be adopted with two herds of elephants if we ever found ourselves in the curious position of wanting to know which of two herds of elephants was the bigger. In this case, however, we should have to find some method of representing elephants—one pebble for each elephant, for example. In counting, however, we use words and those words fulfil the same purpose as pebbles would but are infinitely superior to pebbles not only because they are always available and do not have to be carried around with us in a physical sense but also because they are separately identifiable, as pebbles or other kinds of counter are not. When we are counting, therefore, we are mentally placing the things we are counting on a scale of words, one-to-one. Of course we do not necessarily go up the scale one step at a time, but even if we go up by twos or threes—and few people use larger steps than three unless the objects being counted are not randomly arranged—we still take care to see that the relationship is one-to-one. The process of counting and comparing the two herds of elephants can therefore be represented by the following diagram:

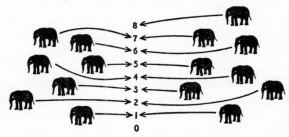

The close connection between this counting diagram and the mapping diagrams reproduced from the Nuffield *Bulletin* is obvious.

It follows from these facts that directedness is inherent in number-words. 'At what stage should a child be introduced to "directed numbers"?' is a question sometimes

asked, meaning at what time should a child be introduced
to the meanings of the plus and minus signs in relation to
the number-scale. The question is not well expressed. It
suggests that there is such a 'thing' as an undirected number—whereas in fact there is not; the directedness is
merely hidden. The very fact that a number-word gets its
meaning from its position on a scale implies direction. In
spoken language the direction is one of *time*; the other kind
of direction—*space*—appears when we give the scale a
visual form. There is no reason why even at the infant
stage the pupils should not be taught the directional
property of plus and minus. To do so is not to put anything very new in their way, for if they have ever played
snakes and ladders—and what child has not?—the experience which will lead to appreciation of the meaning is
already there. There is no reason, therefore, why they
should not at a very early age learn that $+$ means movement 'up' the scale in our convention and $-$ means movement 'down' the scale together with the complementary
directions for the horizontal scale. Nor is there any reason
why they should not learn, through work on a number-
scale, that $3-5=-2$ is as sensible a statement as 'I cannot
give you fivepence because I have only threepence in my
pocket.'

3. The grammar of arithmetic requires rather more
attention than it is sometimes accorded. Since $3+2=5$
and $3\times2=6$ and other such statements are sentences, they
are grammatically structured. A proper attention to this
structure would prevent some looseness of thinking about
many of the elementary statements in arithmetic. For
example, about 60% of primary school teachers regard
$3\times2=6$ as equivalent to $2+2+2=6$; the rest regard it
as equivalent to $3+3=6$. This ambiguity derives from un-
certainty about the grammar of the statement. Does the 2

multiply the 3 or is it multiplied by the 3? The question is a grammatical one. It is an interesting fact that the English Mathematical Association gives a different reading from that of the 60% or so primary school teachers, from that of G. Gattegno, the proponent of the Cuisenaire apparatus in this country, and from that of Catherine Stern designer of the Stern apparatus.

4. A further point needs to be made about sentences in arithmetic. It is that the full understanding of the simplest arithmetical statements requires far more from the pupils than they are customarily asked to give. We have, I hope, come a long way from the days when books or chapters in books were written about the 'number facts' which were to be memorised from tables. If we think of, say, the statement $3+2=5$ not as a 'number fact' but as a sentence to be understood, we shall quickly find ourselves coming to the conclusion that a full understanding of the statement implies the ability to derive from it the following statements: $5=3+2$; $2+3=5$; $5=2+3$; $5-3=2$; $5-2=3\ldots$. The pupil who thoroughly understands the properties of simple numbers will be able to add even to that list. It seems likely that work in deriving statements will form part of the work in the Nuffield scheme because few exercises could be closer to traditional arithmetic and yet at the same time have such a close connection with the structure of arithmetical thinking.

5. In approaching arithmetic and the other branches of mathematics from a linguistic point of view, it is necessary to pay close attention to the nature of abstraction. Several assertions about abstraction have been made in this book. Some of them are particularly relevant here. It was stated, for example, that the most concrete noun is to some extent abstract; the concept of 'dog' is arrived at through experience of a number of individual dogs and through the

experience of differentiating between those animals and other objects of experience. Similarly the concept of 3 — the number not the numeral—is acquired through the experience of perceiving the similarity between groups of three composed of different objects and perceiving the difference between those groups and groups of a different size. The concept of larger numbers is more abstract still. Even as small a number as 9 is more abstract than 3 because a group that size, as we have seen, lies beyond the range of immediate perceptions. It is sometimes said that children who are manipulating numerals, e.g. answering such questions as $6+7=?$, are dealing with abstract numbers, the implication being that the numbers are not abstract when the same question appears in the form: Jack had six marbles and Jim had seven. How many marbles were there altogether? The implication is false. The number-concepts are abstract whether the marbles are mentioned or not.

Although at the later stages of school mathematics much of the work will be a matter of manipulating symbols often with no conscious reference to the meaning of the symbols because both meanings and symbols are so familiar, yet at the earlier stages some representation of the meanings must be provided. It is the great merit of well-designed structural apparatus that it provides a representational background against which the symbols are manipulated. Graphical work, mapping, scale drawing and Venn diagrams all fall into this class of visual representation related to abstract ideas.

Teachers at present have no difficulty in finding advice about how to teach both arithmetic and mathematics at the primary stage or about how to lead children to the discovery of mathematical ideas for themselves. What I have attempted to do in this chapter is merely to explore some of the fundamental ideas mainly from a linguistic point of view. In *Arithmetic in the Decimal Age* I gave a more detailed account of recent ideas about the teaching of arithmetic against its historical background. It is an interesting side-light on the liveliness of the mathematical scene that that book is already in some respects out of date.

I have not appended to this chapter a section on practical applications; for two reasons: 1. For such a section to be of much value on this particular topic would require more detail than it is possible to give within the confines of this book. 2. Such ideas as those incorporated in the Nuffield Project are so new at the primary stage that the methods of presenting them in a satisfactory manner have still to be worked out.

Chapter 8

THE LANGUAGE OF SCIENCE

OCCASIONALLY in the more serious papers and periodicals there breaks out a correspondence about the illiteracy of scientists. Often the 'illiterates' are not scientists at all but students hoping for a career in some field of science, among them a number, no doubt, who were not interested enough in the 'English' they were taught at school to give it serious attention. Sometimes, however, the charges are more serious and are directed not against young students but against experienced writers of books in some branch of science, or of articles published in the specialist journals. In the new edition of 'Fowler', for example, Sir Ernest Gower went to town—modern English usage allows the expression—on what he called 'sociologese' and left his readers in no doubt that in his opinion the minds of many social scientists had fallen under the tyranny of a barbaric tongue of their own invention. A similar view was in the mind of Dr Kathleen Nott, logician, when, writing in *Encounter*, autumn 1964, she used her scalpel on the language used by Dr H. J. Eysenck, psychologist, with such effect that he was moved to reply, with controlled acrimony, in such a way as to imply that his critic had understood neither what he had written nor why it had been necessary for him to write it in that particular way. There appear then to be language problems in science not only for the learner but also for the learned.

I have some hope that in examining the functions of language in science I shall be able to bring together some ideas that will be helpful to teachers with pupils who may have set their minds on a scientific career, to young scientists who are still learning the language of their trade and to anyone who has to read what scientists of various kinds write.

It will, I expect, be accepted that the declared aim of scientists of all kinds is to arrive at objective truth—even a small objective truth. This can be put in a slightly different way—that the scientist's work is a constant endeavour to make statements that will be found to fit the facts by anyone who investigates the statements and the facts with sufficient care, sufficient previous information and the necessary lack of prejudice. It is as well to add here, however, that it is not any fact that the scientist is interested in. Thousands of facts, for example, could be stated about the room I am writing in but hardly any of them would be of interest to a scientist even though they might be just as true as any statement he is likely to make. They are of no interest to him in so far as they have no direct connection with a general law, for what really interests the scientist is the general law that fits the facts and that further facts fit. His aim is to make statements that are true now, were true in the past and will be true in the future. The future to him is perhaps more important than the past for it is in prediction that the scientist's chief power lies. It must also be pointed out here that the ability of the scientist to make statements of the kind described depends very largely upon the precision with which he works. He must think with precision: more and more he must *measure* with precision. In both these activities he is deeply involved with mathematics of one kind or another.

Although very early in this book I suggested that the label idea of language was too simple to fit the facts, it is in the scientific use of language that this idea is least inappropriate. The objection to regarding words as mere labels for things, it will be remembered, was that this idea concealed the fact that between the 'thing' and the name for it came our experience of the 'thing'. Since it is one of the aims of science to cancel out the vagaries of individual experiences, these individual experiences have here less importance and so it is in the sciences that words come nearest to being mere labels. It can be said that part of the scientist's job is to label our material environment. And yet that is only part of the job, necessary because without names for things it is impossible to communicate facts about them, and, what is more important, it is impossible to show their inter-relatedness. It is a commonplace statement about the scientist that he is mapping our material environment. Nowadays he is more likely to be thought of as a shaper rather than a map-maker of the environment. Nevertheless the detailed description of the nature and relatedness of things is an essential preliminary to any prediction about natural forces, whether in the organic or inorganic world, and to all the creative interferences of applied science.

Among the sciences that are most purely map-making is anatomy. Its subject matter is nothing more or less than a description of the various parts of a living organism and where they are situated in relation to one another. Here, for example, is a brief quotation from an anatomical description of the human brain;

The cornu ammonis is situated close to the medial wall of the inferior horn of the lateral ventrical. Since this wall of the hemisphere is thin, there is in the depth of the fissure hippocampi, a continuity between the cornu ammonis proper and the adjacent parts of the cortex, namely the narrow entorhinal and perirhinal formations which on the height of the gyrus hippocampi go over into the temporal areas.

Anyone not familiar with this vocabulary is likely to

find such writing difficult to read and yet the ideas contained in those sentences are no more difficult than those in the following short statement:

'The Trip to Jerusalem is situated under the Castle Rock. It may be reached from the Old Market Square in the centre of the city by way of Friar Lane. . . .'

The increasing load of vocabulary is a problem in many branches of science. The need for a large number of special terms is obvious in such a subject as anatomy, for as more separate 'things' are discovered more names are needed. Aristotle, who thought that the skull was filled merely with a kind of phlegm whose purpose was to keep the body cool, did not require many terms in order to describe the brain as he knew it; he did not even require names for nerve-cells. Today the full anatomical description of the brain alone requires hundreds of special terms. It might be thought that in such a case, if anywhere, there could be devised the kind of language in which the form of the name would be a guide to the nature, or appearance, of the thing named in the sense that two things belonging to the same class would have a name indicating that that was so or that part of the name would serve such a purpose. It may be recalled that in an earlier chapter I discussed the possibility of such a language as the ordinary means of communication and suggested that, a language which was designed with that degree of tidiness would in ordinary usage quickly lose its tidiness because of the inveterate habit human beings have of using metaphor.

The technical language of science, however, hardly encounters this difficulty. Nobody in ordinary life is likely to be speaking in such detail about the brain, for example, as to be using the technical terms in the passage quoted. This remoteness enables scientific language to remain fairly rigidly fixed in its meanings. It also enables the

K

logical design of a language to remain untouched by the vagaries of common usage. The most obvious example of language designed as in itself a logical index is the system worked out in detail, though not invented, by Linnaeus in the field of botany. It is known as the system of 'binomial nomenclature', a system in which the object referred to has a name consisting of two words. In this system normally the first word denotes the genus and the second identifies within the genus e.g. *daphne laureola*. A language of this sort makes the reading of the details of the subject much easier than it otherwise would be because the very act of reading the name brings one more than halfway towards indexing the thing referred to. To those who have learned the meanings of the terms that denote genus, the placing of plants whose botanical names they read is automatic. When, for example, they discover that the genus term in the botanical name of wall-flower is *brassica*, they may be surprised at first but they know that if they examine that delightful spring flower carefully they will see that it has characteristics shared by the cabbage, the cauliflower, the broccoli and the Brussels sprout.

Another aspect of scientific language that lightens the load is its use of meaningful particles in the building up of words. In the anatomical quotation, for example, we find *ento-* and *peri-*. Others will spring readily even to the non-scientific reader's mind: *iso-*, *poly-*, *-itis*, *-osis*, *ifera*, *ectomy*. It has been estimated that there are about a thousand such particles and that the mastery of these would give anyone a scientific vocabulary of tens of thousands of words. Since we have seen that experience of the 'thing' is necessary for the understanding of the word, it is not, however, quite certain that a man's understanding of science would increase at the same rate as the vocabulary he builds up in this Meccano-like way.

Binomial nomenclature and the use of those meaningful particles have certainly made the vocabularies of most sciences more manageable than they would otherwise have been, but, as we shall see in a moment, certain problems of sheer vocabulary still remain.

It is an interesting fact that in the history of scientific terms Chaucer, whom Spenser called 'that well of English undefiled', exerted some influence. He wrote for his little son a kind of scientific dictionary called *A Treatise on the Astrolabe*. As the child knew very little Latin, Chaucer wrote the book in 'naked words in English'. These 'naked' English words were used when the occasion arose to explain words taken from other languages and these imported words were then used in the text of the book. Among the words used by him in this way are *latitude*, *longitude*, *meridian*, *declination*, *equator*, *equinox*, *horizon*, *degrees*, and *minutes* and, from the Arabic *azimuth*, *nadir*, and *zenith*. T. H. Savory in *The Language of Science* claims that these words were brought firmly into English by Chaucer.

Words such as *azimuth* and *nadir* have marked echoes in history. They are indeed technical terms but they echo in the alchemist's den; they go back to the days before science was so vast an undertaking as to require a specifically indexing terminology. Another kind of scientific term is the ordinary everyday word used with a special meaning e.g. *work*, *mass* and *fatigue* (of metals). There are not many of these, but they cause problems in the teaching of elementary science. By far the greatest number of scientific terms, however, are naturally of fairly recent origin. That not all of them fall into the category of logically classifying terms may be seen from the following piece of news and comment that appeared in the *New Scientist* a few years ago:

Taxonomists, people whose concern is with discriminating between various species and the application of a logical system of animal names, have for long used the microscopic structure of the male insect sex organ and its adjacent copulatory hooks as the basis of insect identification. But the student of dragon-flies knows little about ants, the waterbug specialist nothing of microlepidoptera. So there has arisen a fascinating but be-wildering mass of technical terms used in describing male and female mating structure, some 2,000 or so names in Latin, English, French and German. Reduction of this mountain of terms requires two things, first a system of homologies be-tween comparable parts of bug and beetle, moth and mosquito, secondly an agreed international terminology.

The comment went on to congratulate Dr S. L. Tuxen, an eminent Danish authority on silverfish and spring-tails, on managing to edit and get through the press in six and a half years a volume called *A Taxonomist's Glossary of Genitalia in Insects* to which thirty-four writers of many nationalities contributed.

It was not perhaps necessary to prove that the sheer number of scientific terms is itself a problem, but if proof were needed, that is probably it. It may be thought that the labour involved in sorting out such a large vocabulary dealing with such microscopic details hangs on the edge of academic pedantry, but the same commentator went on to forestall that criticism. He wrote:

'For the applied zoologist faced with premature coco-nut fall in the Solomons, with the dreadful problem of native blindness in West Africa, with damage to raspberries in central Scotland, insect taxonomy is the framework upon which his researches and treatment are erected.'

What is that but a statement about the importance not only of precision in map-making but of the desirability that as far as possible the detailed characteristics of the map should be reflected in the vocabulary.

The view of science and scientific language that I have so far presented makes it all seem a fairly simple matter, the only difficulty that of the increasing load of vocabulary that the discovery of more and more 'things' makes inevitable. That is a reasonable way of looking at a purely descriptive science like anatomy. But most scientists are engaged in the study not only of dead organs but of living organisms or of interacting forces and so his task is the complex one very often of making true statements about one factor in a complicated process. Complex situations are those in which many events are simultaneously reacting. It follows that there is no event which it is impossible to regard as complex. Simplicity is more likely to be found in the language which purports to describe an event than in the event itself. *The shadows lengthened as the day wore on* is a very simple statement, but behind it lie the theories of light, of relativity, of the earth's motion, of the sources of the sun's energy, of perception. There is, it is true, no need to understand any of these theories in order to understand the sentence. The statement occurs in Greek literature somewhere I have no doubt and the writer of it then had only the most naïve ideas of the various theories mentioned. But we today are more aware, or ought to be more aware, of how much may be left out when simple statements are made.

It is not the mere number of events that produces complexity but also what we might call the contrariness of events, when forces work against one another. It is, for example, fairly easy to describe in straightforward language the physical movements of a regimented squad of soldiers on parade, but it is quite impossible to put into words an account of the actions of each individual soldier in the confusion of a battle. Take a much smaller body of men—two football teams. The sports writer could not possibly note and remember what every member of even one of the teams did during the game, but must be content with some general statements and the recording of a few highlights. It is this contrariness of events that make prediction difficult. We have already noted that part of the scientist's interest in formulating general laws is that on the basis of these laws he will be able to make statements that are true of events in the future. Millions of people are reminded every week of the extreme difficulty of predicting what will happen when twenty-two men meet on a football field. In the language of the scientist: *There are too many variables*.

Teachers on the whole are very well aware of situations in which there are too many variables for prediction to be accurate. They are aware of the vast amount of time and energy expended in the attempt to predict the future academic achievements of pupils. Our concern is not with techniques of assessment or the reliability and validity of tests, but with the function of language in these complex situations. Since certainty of prediction is not possible in these situations, the only language the scientist can use is the language of probability, but he does not use the everyday language of probability like—*on the whole, there is a chance that, it is just possible that, hardly likely*. He uses instead, as every teacher very well knows, the language of statistics, a branch of arithmetic in which the chief concern is to give a measure of probability. Statistical techniques can be exceedingly complicated and may also involve a vast amount of tabulation and computation. This labour has been greatly reduced in recent years by the use of calculating machines and computers, but the difficulty of prediction where there are many variables still remains.

Sometimes it is not a very difficult matter to arrange an experimental situation so that a variable is, so to speak, isolated. In the testing of a new fertiliser, for example, the individual variations between seeds is cancelled out by taking a sufficient number of seeds on which the new chemical compound is to be used and a comparable number on which it is not to be used. By taking sufficient numbers and due care with the siting and soil of the groups to be compared, other variables will be cancelled out too — accidents such as the fact that one seed may land on a pebble below the surface that impedes root development, attack by grubs or disease.

The size of the 'sufficient number' can be calculated but in many statistical investigations — indeed in most — the mere size of the number is not the only thing to be taken into account. For example, if it is required to know how well a particular television programme is being received by the public in general, the opinions of seven million teen-agers would not give as true a picture as the opinions of ten thousand viewers of different ages, income groups and general environment.

One of the key terms in statistics is 'correlation'. This is usually given as a numeral with a plus or minus sign in front of it. To say that there is a correlation of $+1$ between two variables is to say that the correlation is perfect, e.g. the weight of a load and the amount of energy expended in taking it up a hill. A correlation of -1 is the opposite; there is, for example, a nearly perfect negative correlation between the amount of electricity used in street lighting and the number of hours of daylight: it is not absolutely perfect because occasionally street lights are switched on in dense fog. It is almost a mis-use of language, however, to speak of 'perfect correlation' because most instances of it are either man-made or obvious. By man-made I mean the kind of perfect correlation one gets, say, between the revenue from a tobacco tax and the value of the tobacco sold legitimately; the one is calculated from the other so that the perfect correlation is a *made* one. Language can play curious tricks with correlations, however. I have heard given as an example of perfect correlation the amount of sunshine and the absence of cloud during the hours of daylight. Since, however, absence of cloud virtually means sunshine, this is rather like saying that an event is perfectly correlated with itself. Alternatively one could question how much of the sky was being taken into account, for it is quite possible for a quarter of the sky to be cloud-covered though seen from a position where the sun was shining all the time. No, 'perfect correlation' is not a very meaningful term; the concept of perfect correlation is significant merely as the two ends of the scale, the ends where probability becomes certainty and the language of probability is no longer applicable.

It is sometimes said that you can prove anything by means of statistics; it might be truer to say that you can hardly prove anything without statistics. Certainly today when attempts are being made to apply measuring techniques to the complicated behaviour of human groups the only possible measurements are measurements implying probability. Even the *comparatively* simple problem of discovering whether or not the smoking of cigarettes causes cancer of the lung has been a statistical battleground for years—even among disinterested statisticians. Those who demand certainty in every scientific statement will not find it in statements involving many interacting factors. Even in the sciences that are called exact, certainty is not all that easy to come by as every schoolboy knows when he compares the results of his experiments with those he is supposed to get according to the book: the percentage of air in water, for example, never seems to accord with what the book says. It is a strange paradox, too, that the more precise science becomes, the more evident it is that scientific statements are essentially statistical. No atom, for example, can be assumed to be identical with any other atom without infringing 'truth', for since atoms according to current theory are structures of energy moving in space and time, identity between two atoms would imply that the particles of energy occupy the same space at the same time—and how then could there be two atoms? In the days of the scholastics arguments went on about such matters as how many angels could be balanced on the point of a pin. My present argument may seem to be of that calibre. but it has two aims: 1. To show how easy it is to arrive at the irreconcilable by means of a logical argument; 2. To show that it is not wholly fantastic to say that the results of an exact science like chemistry are statistical in the sense that it describes the *average* behaviour of large masses of atoms and molecules. If it is argued that all atoms or molecules of a particular substance are identical in their behaviour, then it will have to be explained why when water boils some molecules burst free from the liquid mass and some do not, why in the sea there are some molecules that have collected an extra hydrogen atom and many more that have not . . . and a whole lot of other similar whys.

In spite of the ubiquity of statistical language, in spite of its presence where it is sometimes least expected, in spite of the fact that the aim of statistics is to give as great precision as possible to statements involving probability, it can hardly be said that in all sciences the evolution of statistical techniques has been accompanied by progress commensurate with the amount of labour involved in applying them. The history of education, for example, does not provide many instances of advance as a result of the application of statistical techniques to educational problems. What does stand out clearly is that the application of statistical techniques to educational problems has not only been largely a waste of the statistician's time—apart from any enjoyment he may have got out of it—but had also resulted in a greater waste of time by others. The I.Q. was, for example, a statistical abstraction; it came to be regarded as virtually a real thing. Reams of research work were published establishing the principle that the I.Q. was fixed by nature; educational systems were adapted to fit the concept; it was 'proved' that intelligence ceased to develop about the age of 16. This period was followed by a period during which a similar amount of energy was devoted to research that 'proved' most previous research to be wrong; the I.Q. was no longer fixed by heredity; educational organisation need no longer be designed to fit the concept of fixed intelligence. In the teaching of reading the waste products of statistical research have piled up perhaps even higher. Here, however, it is rather more noticeable that the techniques of science have been used as instruments of persuasion.

Probably the main reason why statistical research has been so fruitless in the field of education is that the language of statistics is based upon the behaviour of groups whereas education is concerned with individuals. We all know that the term 'average' is abstract and may have little connection with the details of a situation. For example, two groups of the same average age may be very different in respect of the individuals composing the groups: one group may consist of mothers and children, the other entirely of teenagers. It is not often that a statistician will use a simple average; he has devised a language which will take into account the differences between groups that the simple average will describe as being identical. What he cannot do, however, is to say anything about an individual child except in relation to a group and in so doing he must select some aspect of the individual in respect of which he can be compared to the group, leaving out most of what makes the individual what he is. It follows that great care must be taken in reading statistical conclusions; they are fairly high up on the ladder of abstraction and in reading such language it is necessary to consider what has been left out as well as what has been kept in.

The sad history of statistics in the educational world is to some extent due also to the overlooking of the fact that the language of statistics merely describes a situation in a particular way. An experiment that is badly designed cannot be patched up by statistical treatment of the results; the most that can be hoped for is that the weakness may be concealed, as rust may be concealed by spraying a car. In educational matters the number of variables to be dealt with is usually so great that a small piece of experimental work may produce a vast mountain of statistical analysis in the course of which the plain facts of the case get lost. An investigation into the efficacy of methods of teaching reading, for example, will involve the home background of the groups of children being compared—how is that to be measured? By the rateable value of the houses on the assumption that the better the home in the material sense the better the intellectual environment? *There* is an abstraction, if you like. It will involve the skill of the teachers —what measure can be given to that? Experience? Intelligence? Sympathy? Can these be measured? Small wonder that most statistical investigations into methods of teaching reading support the hypothesis the researchers started out with. Like attendance at lectures, the main result is to confirm the seekers after truth in their own prejudices.

In the often-quoted Scottish report *Selection for Secondary Education* there occurs this quaint confession:

'We started with nearly 1,000 correlations. These have been condensed to 8 . . . and then expanded to 30. In performing this condensation, we may, at times, have taken a little statistical licence, but Table XXXII is worthy of respect in consideration of the labour involved in its preparation.'

Statistical language is sometimes used, not always deliberately, in such a way as to produce an impression of great care and exactitude. For example, in his *Backwardness in the Basic Subjects* (Oliver and Boyd) Professor F. J. Schonell has these sentences:

'Although each word has its characteristic configuration, it would seem that young children are easily led astray in their early reading by similarity of configuration. There is a correlation of $0.806–0.02$ between errors due to this factor and total errors made?

To the semi-statistical reader there is a certain magic in the precision here—to the third decimal place! It is not easy in the face of such formidable accuracy to realise that all the errors referred to could be due not to that factor at all but to something near the opposite—too great attention to similar details in the printed words.

One fact that works against the satisfactory use of statistics is that the statistician is often a specialist called in to work upon material for which he has not initial responsibility, and sometimes he has no overt responsibility for the interpretation put upon his work. The result may be that the statistical section of a report has only a spurious connection with scientific statement.

Although it is true that anything that is written or

spoken must be written or spoken in a certain way and that therefore it is impossible to escape from having some kind of style, yet the only style suitable for scientific reporting is that which presents the facts and the conclusions in such a way that the reader has no difficulty in reading those precise facts and conclusions into them. The premiss of his whole work is that facts are sacred. His style then must bow to the facts; there can be no question of writing them up, putting on the fancy dress of 'style' or making them seem of greater consequence than they are. The processes being described may be complicated, but the language should not be more complicated than the bare truth demands. It will possibly be necessary to use statistical arguments, but they too should be no more elaborate than the facts and conclusions of their nature demand. That is how it should be; how it *is* is another matter:

Here is a paragraph from an article in the *American Journal of Psychology*:

Safe and efficient driving is a matter of living up to the psychological laws of locomotion in a spatial field. The driver's field of safe travel and his minimum stopping zone must accord with the objective possibilities; and a ratio greater than unity must be maintained between them. This is the basic principle. High speed, slippery road, night-driving, sharp curves, heavy traffic and the like are 'dangerous', when they are, because they lower the field-zone ratio.

'Sometimes,' wrote T. H. Savory in *The Language of Science*, 'it is difficult to believe that the writing in some scientific reports is seriously meant.' This is such an occasion. The writer of ordinary English would be content to say that the safe driver will not drive so fast that he cannot pull up in time when he meets a dangerous situation.

It would be easy to produce a fat anthology of linguistic curiosities compiled from scientific reports, but I have no intention of piling on the agony. For three short paragraphs that appeared in the periodical *Human Relations* I have, however, a particular affection. The amount of scientific jargon is moderate enough to beguile us into thinking something of some moment may be being said and the sentences are short enough to allow us to think that plain communication is being attempted, and yet the total effect is . . . well, here is the passage:

There are non-social restraints which make it difficult or even impossible to change one's ability. These non-social restraints are largely absent for opinions.

If a person changes his mind about something, deserts one belief in favour of another, there is no further difficulty in the way of consummating the change. It is true that there are sometimes considerable difficulties in getting someone to change his mind concerning an opinion or belief. Such resistance may arise because of consistency with other opinions or beliefs, personality characteristics that make a person lean in one direction or another, and the like. But the point to be stressed is that once these resistances are overcome, there is no further restraint which would make it difficult for the change to become effective.

There are generally strong non-social restraints, however, against changing one's ability, or changing one's performance which reflects that ability. Even if a person is convinced that he should be able to run faster or should be more intelligent, and even if he is highly motivated to improve his ability in this respect, there are greater difficulties in the way of consummating the change.

Does this say anything more than, You can change your mind but you cannot add an inch to your stature by taking thought?

One of the characteristics of bad style in scientific writing in English is the use of Germanic grammatical constructions instead of plain English ones, as seen in the piling up of qualifying words, not necessarily adjectival in form, in front of nouns. Dr J. R. Baker, in an interesting article on this subject (*The Use of English Vol VIII No. 1*) quoted 'adenosine triphosphate activated actomyosin contraction' as an outstanding example of this—the meaning in English: 'the contraction of actomyosin, activated by adenosine triphosphate'. There the meaning was clear despite the un-English construction. This clarity is not always present. The writer of the phrase 'iron containing globules' did not, for example, mean iron that contained globules but globules that contained iron.

One of the sad tricks the human mind plays upon itself when it is engaged in the attempt to describe the unmeasurable in scientific terms is to invent names and then treat the names as though they were things. *Entities are not to be multiplied with necessity*, wrote William of Occam many centuries ago. There are occasions, however, when, in reading texts in the social sciences, we begin to wonder whether whole sciences have not been erected upon the contrary principle. It looks sometimes as though the multiplication of entities forms the basis of this or that branch of social science. This characteristic is not confined to the unknown strugglers for recognition. A fine example occurs in the writings of Freud. One of the remarkable things about Freud is the contrast between his early work and that of his mature years. While still a young man, he wrote, and published at his own expense, a short work called *Aphasia* in which he surveyed and very clearly summarised previous work on the neuro-pathology of language with acute comments and contributions of his own. The work by which he made his name, however, did not have the same clarity nor did it remain so close to the observable data. His manner of thought was to suspect, from evidence, the existence of a set of events to which a name could be given, to invent or adapt a name for that set of events and then to assume that because there was now a name the events had no longer a merely suspected existence but an actual one. Bernard Lonergan, S. J. in his Thomistic survey of modern thought entitled *Insight* comments on this aspect of Freud's work: 'On many occasions Freud represents the outlook of his time and tends to regard observable psychic events as appearance and unobservable entities as reality.'

Freud's description of *libido*, one of his key terms, very well illustrates this characteristic of Freud's thinking and is a good example of technical terms running riot:

We have defined the concept of libido as a quantitatively variable force which could serve as a measure of processes and transformations occurring in the field of sexual excitation. We distinguish this libido in respect of its special origin from the energy which must be supposed to underlie mental processes in general, and we thus also attribute a qualitative character to it. In thus distinguishing between libidal and other forms of psychic energy we are giving expression to the presumption that the sexual processes occurring in the organism are distinguished from the nutritive processes by a special chemistry. . . . We thus reach the idea of a quantity of libido, to the mental representation of which we give the name ego-libido. . . . This ego-libido is conveniently accessible to analytic study only when it becomes object-libido. . . . We can then perceive it concentrating upon objects, becoming fixated upon them, or abandoning them, moving from one object to another, and, from these situations, directing the subject's sexual activity, which leads to the satisfaction, that is to the partial and temporary extinction, of the libido. . . . We can follow the object-libido through still further vicissitudes. When it is withdrawn from the object, it is held in suspense in peculiar conditions of tension and is finally drawn back into the ego, so that it becomes ego-libido once again. In contrast to object-libido, we also describe ego-libido as 'narcissistic' libido. . . .

So here is something which is quantitatively variable and yet could serve as a measure, but when we think of it quantitatively we give it another name. By some sleight of mind this turns it into another thing. At the same time, even after it has become this other thing, there is hardly anything we can say about it because it is not conveniently accessible to analysis until it becomes something else. . . .

This seems to me a clear case of words creating 'things'.

I may have given the impression that the sciences, and particularly the inexact sciences, are a clutter of words. If they were so, they would not be as effective as we see them in the world around us. It is among the writings of the inexact scientists, however, —if we omit the politicians and advertising men—that we find the most compelling examples of language distorted and distorting. No politician would ever reach a position of power if he told the truth, the whole truth and nothing but the truth, nor, if he began to do so when in power, would he retain his position for long. Even if it were possible for him to do so, even if he could find the language, there are always questions of national interest which call for a withholding of the answers. There is an open conspiracy among the adults of any population which accepts the politician's right not to be frank and free in his speech even when he is asking the populace 'to face the brutal facts'. The advertising men on the other hand are committed to the truth only to the extent that if they stray too far away from it the products will not sell. The scientist, however, is committed to the truths that he has discovered and in so far as he is good at his job his language will fit the facts, the entities will not be multiplied beyond necessity.

How pleasant it is to report that no language could be clearer than Sir Frederick Bartlett's in *Thinking* and that the 'behavioral' scientists of America in a symposium called *Contemporary Approaches to Creative Thinking* (Ed. W. E. Henry, Atherton Press, 1962) can produce a series of studies in which, though the matter is complicated, the language is clear.

THE PRACTICAL ASPECT

In The *Excitement of Writing* A. B. Clegg maintains that the ability to write is indivisible and by that he meant that if a pupil is good at 'creative writing' he will also be good at writing up scientific experiments. He implies, too, that it is better for pupils, at the primary stage at least, to be allowed to write, stimulated to write, about what matters to them most. I have not the slightest doubt that this is so. Now that science is coming into the primary school, the last thing one wants to see is the formal writing up of scientific experiments in the narrow inhibiting way that is not uncommon at the secondary stage. Science in the primary school is better as active inquiry with plenty of speech and very little writing—unless a pupil wants to write about something he has discovered. I have an idea that pupils would get more fun—once shown how to go about it—writing about what they do not know about, say, the wind—and then trying to find answers to the questions that arise than they would by writing the answers to the questions. In any case there is no such thing as 'a language of science' at the primary school level, there is merely writing and speaking.

I should think that every pupil at the secondary stage of schooling should have discussed the questions that arise in this chapter, though a considerable amount of simplifcation would be required. One of the paradoxes about this whole business is, however, that when scientists write for schools they usually make a better job of it than when they are writing for other scientists.

Chapter 9

THE LANGUAGE OF POETRY

I HAVE called this chapter 'The Language of Poetry' and yet I will not necessarily be concerned solely with the kind of writing in which most of the lines fall short of the margin. As far as this book is concerned, the world of language revolves between the poles of science and poetry. Some of the linguistic features of the hemisphere of science were discussed in the previous chapter; in this chapter I shall do much the same with the other hemisphere, the hemisphere into which falls any piece of writing which does not set out to be scientific or even true according to the definition a scientist would give to 'truth'.

The territory to be explored in one chapter, then, is vast; whole libraries have been devoted to the exploration of parts of it. There is a chance, therefore, that a short chapter dealing with so long a topic will amount to no more than a collection of general statements. The safeguard against so disappointing a result is the limiting effect of the context of this book. Non-scientific writing will be discussed here in the light of the theory of communication that has been argued out in the main body of the book. Most works of literary criticism are written on the assumption that meaning and feeling are *transferred* from one mind to another. The assumption is not always explicitly stated; but it can be read not only into the spaces between the lines but also into the spaces between the words. There is a possibility then that even the commonplaces of literary criticism may have a fresh look when examined in the light of the contrary assumption.

It will be convenient to begin with the kind of writing that is of all writing furthest from the statements of science. The characteristic of such writing is that it has no meaning in the scientific sense at all—so little meaning of any kind that it would hardly seem to matter whether meaning was transferred from the originating mind or not.

Here is an extract from such a poem; Ben Jonson's 'Hymn to Diana':

> Queen and huntress, chaste and fair,
>   Now the sun is laid to sleep,
> Seated in thy silver chair,
>   State in wonted manner keep:
> Hesperus entreats thy light,
>   Goddess excellently bright. . . .

That poem was one of a number selected for reading by the Irish poet, James Stephens, some years ago in a radio programme called 'Pure Poetry'. Readers will no doubt be able to recall many poems or parts of poems that say as little as the 'Hymn to Diana'. A. E. Housman gave a similar example in a famous lecture called 'The Nature of Poetry'.

Anyone listening to James Stephens's reading of Jonson's poem could have had no doubt of the affinity of this kind of poetry with music. The last thing a scientist is concerned with is speech, or the sounds of words as imagined in inner speech; sound, however, is intrinsic in poetry. This is not to say that a poet must always be writing what is pleasant to the ear, but it is to say that the name 'poet' can only be a courtesy title when applied to someone who writes what sets out to be poetry without paying attention to how it sounds when spoken; the music may be harsh, but it will be there. There is no 'meaning', in the 'labelling' sense, in music—except, arguably, in what is quaintly called 'programme music' and in such sound-effects as the call of the cuckoo and the tumult of the storm in Beethoven's 'Pastoral Symphony'. The 'pure poetry' of Jonson's lines is not founded, however, upon nonsense syllables; it is not a matter of slithy toves gyring and gimbling in the wabe. All the words are to be found in the dictionary and they are put together in an order that seems to make sense; they are grammatically organised, syntactically unambiguous. But what do they say? Just enough to keep us from thinking that they are meaningless. Indeed if you start thinking about the meaning, the poetry goes— momentarily; we can easily bring it back again by letting logic slide.

There is a word 'chair'; we know its various meanings. There is a word 'silver'; with its ordinary meanings we are also familiar. But let those two words come together in the context of Jonson's poem and something very peculiar happens; the ordinary meanings do not matter; they are a mere basis from which to escape into the world of music. The context transforms them.

This power of the context is not peculiar to poetry. We have seen in the analysis of the dynamics of communication how there is a continual interaction between the various elements involved, but the *linguistic* context becomes especially powerful in poetry. In scientific writing, as we have seen, the word is as near being a label for the 'thing' as it ever can be; in this kind of poetry it is hardly even a label for the experience of the thing; it is removed from the world of ordinary meanings, ceases to be a 'dictionary' word, one might say, and becomes—what? A musical note or phrase? In a sense, yes. But we cannot think of it as a separate note or phrase. Sunlight is no longer sunlight when it is broken in a prism. In science the meanings of names are important even when taken separately;

in poetry of this kind the language is organic. Take the words out of the organic context and the poem comes to pieces in our hands. 'Entangled in a net of thoughtless delight' was Housman's description of the effect poetry of this kind had on him—and should have, he thought, on other people.

The language of poetry produces many other types of experience, but this one—delight regardless of meaning—lies near the heart of it all. Johnson said that any attempt to define poetry merely showed the narrowness of the definer, but he also said that like light, which was equally impossible to define, he knew it when he met it. The man who will not recognise poetry of this kind when he meets it is the one who tries to put meanings of the ordinary kind in it. We have seen that looking for meanings in another person's words is a matter of referring to our own experiences and usually reorganising them in some way. It is a characteristic of poetry of this kind, however, that the attempt to put meanings in is a waste of effort and a rejection of what the poet has to give—'thoughtless delight'.

If this 'thing' we have been discussing is 'pure poetry', then the usual commonplace about the poet being subjective and the scientist objective, if taken in the usual sense, has very little connection with poetry in its quintessential form. There is nothing *personal* about the 'Hymn to Diana', no expression of personal emotions, nothing but delight in the music that can be made with words. The scientist who takes pleasure in loading his sentences with technical terms in order to inflate his report is being as personal as Jonson who is writing up nothing in such a way as to produce music and is taking pleasure in it—and the same is true of the more mature scientist who takes a pleasure in finding the statements that will fit the facts.

I have called this 'pure poetry'. In so doing I do not mean to suggest that this is the greatest poetry; I am merely following James Stephens, but at the same time am led to do so by the thought that 'pure poetry', being in the ordinary sense meaningless, is most remote from the good scientific report or plain prose statement. We have seen that bad scientific writing can be in effect meaningless. Lack of meaning therefore is not the essential characteristic.

This sort of poetry is clearly a very limited thing; it is remote from the ordinary business of living, from the anxieties and joys, the doubts and certainties, the frustrations and achievements, the love and hate, the eagerness and ennui that are the pattern into which the detailed events of our days fall. It would take a lot of probably specious argument to fit such poetry into Matthew Arnold's definition of poetry as 'a criticism of life' and no argument, however specious, could fit in into Wordsworth's definition, 'the spontaneous overflow of powerful feelings'.

Limited though poetry of this kind may be, the effect which it produces in the mind seems to me to be an essential part of the experience of poetry. What kind of an effect is it? Housman described his physical symptoms — a bristling of the skin, shivers down the spine, a constriction of the throat, a precipitation of water to the eyes, and a feeling which he said he could only describe by borrowing a phrase from one of Keats's letters, where, referring to Fanny Brawne, that poet wrote, 'everything that reminds me of her goes through me like a spear'. The physical symptoms are side-effects. The effect on the mind — which of course cannot be entirely separated from the body — can, I think, be described in one word *elation*, the same sort of elation that music may bring. Can anything be said about it except that it happens? Two things can perhaps be said—apart from the general statement that the 'music' of it is important: 1. The fitness of it all is a source of delight (see the chapter on 'Thinking'), 2. There is an unenvious admiration that anyone could work such magic. This second point possibly requires further explanation. The work of art which does not in our opinion succeed leaves us with a feeling of dissatisfaction; a promise was not fulfilled. The mere fact that we are aware that it did not come off indicates that somewhere in our minds there was an expectancy—vague but to us real. Where the work of art does come off, it does more than fulfil our expectancy; it surprises us by exceeding what we thought possible. This surprise at a fulfiment beyond our vague expectations is one of the causes of the elation.

And what has this to do with the theory of communication I have been expounding? This, I think. In the case of poetry so slenderly connected with ordinary meanings it is as though the poet had said: 'You know, and I know, the dreadful separateness of human beings. We know the impossibility of full understanding between people. Your meanings and not my meanings. To hell with meanings then, here is joy.'

There is, then, a joyous way of saying nothing, language which elates but does not inform, a way of writing which is sufficient in itself. To say this is not to subscribe to the theory of art for art's sake. Let us say, rather, art for the sake of joy.

Poetry, however, is a many-splendoured thing. The elation I speak of may be the mark of essential poetry, but the presence of the power to elate does not depend on the absence of ordinary meanings. 'Thoughtless delight' is not the only kind of delight that poetry brings. Indeed part of the fascination of it all, and part of the delight, comes from the alternations of balance between the meaningful and the meaningless—the 'meaningful' being that into which we can, we feel, legitimately put our meanings, and the meaningless that into which no meanings are to be put. There are in most poems lines or passages into which we can put ordinary prose meanings and others as in the Jonson poem where such meanings are an intrusion.

Here are two lines which I have found elative and which are interesting in this connection:

> Tell me now, did dawn come first or roses,
> Or did the Cyprian stain them from one shell?

The simple fact behind those lines is that sometimes the sky is red at dawn. But what a silly question? We all know, don't we, that there were innumerable dawns before there ever was a rose. And what about the Cyprian staining the skies with dye extracted from sea-shells! What utter nonsense. And yet those lines can be elative. Why? Here it is not so wholly the music, lovely in sound though the lines are. There is something more and it is connected with an aspect of language mentioned in the chapter on 'The Dynamics of Communication', the power of associative ideas, the unbuckling of the mind from the fetters of logic. Horizons open up upon vistas of time. Imagine a dawn before the time of roses, before the time of any plant . . . sea-shells: life in the sea before there were roses on land . . . the multifarious varieties of sea-shells. . . . fishers in the Mediterranean at dawn . . . and the dawn of civilisation in the Mediterranean region . . . dawns before recorded time, dawn in the early syllables of the records.

Those lines are a translation by Helen Waddell of a fragment of a medieval Latin poem and are quoted by her, just those two lines of poetry in a page of prose, in *Wandering Scholars*. It may be objected that the writer of that fragment could not possibly have had in his mind the ideas that arose in my mind when I read the poem. Even if he had heard of Anaximander's primitive theory of evolution, life rising from the sea, he could not have thought in the terms in which it is impossible not to think since the days of Darwin. That does not matter. To say that it does is to say that the poet is writing plain matter of fact. The important thing is that the enlarging effect is there. 'A theatre opened up within my brain,' wrote De Quincey of his opium dreams. Something like that happened with me when that fragment burst forth upon the page of prose—but no, a theatre is too enclosed a thing. It was as though the curtains of time itself had parted. Possibly the lines were more powerful because of the context—medieval scholarship, a fragment, the ruin affecting the imagination more strongly than the thing intact.

What meaning did Coleridge want his readers to put into his phrase 'the willing suspension of disbelief'? Surely this—that when he has been successful with us, the poet persuades us to let the literal truth go and accept what he says as being more important than the plain statement of fact. Sometimes he is so successful in this persuading that we are not even aware that the literal truth has gone but continue to imagine it is in the poet's words. Here is a short poem by Edward Thomas.

Tall Nettles

Tall nettles cover up, as they have done
   These many springs, the rusty harrow, the plough
Long worn out, and the roller made of stone:
   Only the elm-butt tops the nettles now.

This corner of the farmyard I like most:
   As well as any bloom upon a flower
I like the dust on the nettles, never lost
   Except to prove the sweetness of a shower.

This we might say is poetry with the accent of prose. It is straightforward, an accurate description, photographic one might say, though done by an expert photographer capable of selecting and composing the details he needs. And yet we feel that it is not plain descriptive prose; that there is something in the quality of it that does not belong to the world of plain statement. There is indeed plain meaning here in plenty. But there is more; there is an intricate musical pattern which it would be boring to analyse but which can hardly escape anyone who reads the poem aloud with care. And the elation? Here, for me, it comes at the end, a quiet elation it is true, but there nevertheless in the words:

> . . . the dust on the nettles, never lost
> Except to prove the sweetness of a shower.

Not from these words only does the elation spring but from those words *in that context*, for their strength comes in part from the matter-of-fact statements that have gone before. Those last two lines are from the matter-of-fact point of view utter nonsense. Dust settles on nettles; sometimes rain washes the dust off. These are the plain facts as near as ordinary language can put them, though no doubt a scientific report of some complicated length could be written about how it comes about that the water does manage to wash the dust off.

What then has happened? Some very curious things. First we accept the nonsense lines as being a particularly vivid way of describing a plain fact, as giving one more detail of a vivid picture. Then almost immediately we realise that this is a detail from our own experience— the whole freshness of the countryside after rain is revealed in that simple statement about rain on nettles. It is *our* experience; this is how we really have seen it though we have never quite thought of it like that before. It fits, and because it fits so well we never again look at the dust on nettles with quite the same eyes. But much of this does not come into consciousness. We do not analyse our experience but accept it gratefully.

And yet behind all this lies the truth of the objective-subjective generality about the relationship between science and poetry. What Edward Thomas has given us here is *his* picture of a corner of a farmyard. What he has told us in the final lines is how the rain on dusty nettles appears to *him*. If he is successful, it is also how it appears to us. We then know it to be a true statement about a detail of experience.

Scientists on the whole believe that they are *the* truth-tellers. Some will maintain that scientific truth is the only truth. That it is not so is readily proved. Water, they define as H_2O — but what has H_2O to do with the rain on the dusty nettles? Or, to bring the thing nearer to the scientist's heart and bosom — what has H_2O to do with the rainy weather that spoils his holiday or the showers that after a drought bring life to his garden. The chemical formula is a generality and is therefore abstract; it omits the particulars of life, but these are to a large extent what the poet is concerned with. Every moment is unique. It is the uniqueness of experiences that the poet is chiefly interested in and, whether it is his conscious intention or not, he speaks to give these experiences a unique expression. There is here a conflict not only between the scientific statement and the poetic statement but also between the elementary nature of language and the statements of poetry, because the whole classifying function of language is built up upon the ignoring of differences. Human beings, classifying unique experiences by means of language and thus washing out differences, have used this analogical framework to build up elaborate systems of thought. But classification implies also an acknowledgement of differences. Every potato is different from all other potatoes, but normally we think about them as being the same and in doing so we imply their differences from other things — vegetable, animal or mineral. The poet will reverse this process. He will call the moon a potato if it suits his purpose, and, in the proper context we accept that statement as a statement of a kind of truth.

Here are two lines of poetry which show a slightly different relationship between the languages of fact and fancy from that which we have so far discussed. In their context the lines mean that it is not necessary to be a man of action, to be obviously doing things, in order to exert an influence upon the course of human events, that there are people who merely by being what they are exert this influence; even though—'innocent'—they are unaware of it. Here, now, are the lines:

> The innocent moon that nothing does but shine
> Moves yet the labouring surges of the world.

Here there are clearly two levels of meaning. There lies behind the words the plain prose fact that the gravitational pull of the moon upon the oceans causes the tides. But that fact is merely a sort of carrier-wave upon which is superimposed the meaning made explicit above. Why does he not say in plain terms what he means? For the simple reason that the plain terms will not say what he means.

It is often stated—particularly in schools—that the best English style is the plain direct one. For many purposes it is. In scientific reporting the best style is *always* that which is as plain, as direct and as unambiguous as the necessary technical vocabulary will allow it to be. The plain direct style is fitting for the purposes of exposition—as in this book. But even here it has its dangers, for though it may be true that simplicity is a vital quality in explanatory writing, it has its dangers. It may be that in his search for the simple statement a writer may avoid complicated questions and treat his subject-matter more superficially than the truth requires. And again writing that is always explicit may fail to engage the attention of the reader because it is all too easy. The strength of the indirect statement and the symbolic statement lies in the fact that they make a double-pronged attack on the reader's attention; the mind is engaged, so to speak, at different levels. There is furthermore the element of surprise, surprise that words which say one thing should mean that other thing, and if the two things surprisingly *fit* there may come the elation. Along with these elements there is the heightening effect of the music of the words, a music which derives not merely from the metrical beat with its variations but also from the sound-patterns intrinsic in continuous language. In the lines quoted, for example, it is not without significance that the sound represented by the letter 'n' runs through the whole of the first line but appears not at all in the second, or that the second word in the first line 'innocent' is in such sharp contrast to the second word in the next 'yet', or that both are in such contrast in sound to all the other words in the lines.

The alternations of balance in poetry are not merely between the meaningful and the meaningless nor even between fact and fancy, but also between the explicit and the implicit, the direct and the indirect statement. Dylan Thomas wrote a poem which he called 'Among those Killed in the Dawn Raid was a Man Aged a Hundred'. This poem begins:

When the morning was waking over the war
He put on his clothes and stepped out and he died,

The locks yawned loose and a blast blew them wide,
He dropped where he loved on the burst pavement stone
And the funeral grains of the slaughtered floor.

Nothing could be more explicit than the first two lines. The third line seems explicit in itself, but unexpected in the context and then it becomes clear that, though the statement about the locks yawning loose describes one of those vivid details that make a scene live, it is also a statement about death: life is no longer locked in the body. 'He dropped where he loved on the burst pavement stone' is also as explicit as the simplest prose, but again the compression of the statement is such that, through the echoes of inner speech if we are reading the poem silently, 'loved' means 'lived and loved' and then, in the last line quoted in this poem about an 'ancient', there is an echo of the ancient custom of burying grains of corn with the corpse for the soul's journey.

I began this discussion of the language of poetry with some thoughts on thoughtless poetry and showed that poetry can be made out of what is *plainly* nonsense. We accept, or indeed ignore, the nonsense because we are not looking for sense; it is enough that we delight in the music.

Another kind of nonsense appears when the balance between the implicit and the explicit is weighted too heavily against the explicit. Here are some lines from another of Dylan Thomas's poems:

Altarwise by owl-light in the half-way house
The gentleman lay graveward with his furies;
Abaddon in the hangnail cracked from Adam,
And, from his fork, a dog among the fairies,
The atlas-eater with a jaw for news,
Bit out the mandrake with tomorrow's scream.

These are the first lines of a poem called 'Altarwise by owl-light.' Whatever else may be true about them, it is

certainly a fact that they can be read as nonsense and that
that is how ninety-nine people out of a hundred will read
them. But what kind of nonsense is it? The nonsense of
the 'Hymn to Diana' did not trouble us. This nonsense
may do because it is not easy to get rid of the feeling that
the expenditure of so much serious energy must surely
indicate that something of significance is being said. So we
begin to search and then—unless we are specialists in
literature rather than life—give up while the mystery is
still dark around us.

'Poetry must astonish by a fine excess,' wrote Keats,
but there is a limit even to excess. Communication in the
sense that thought and feeling come from the outside and
are not generated within may be impossible, but not even
the poet can escape from the necessity of writing in such a
way as to create the situation in which it is *as though* the
thought and feeling had come across in the words. It might
indeed be argued that the very distinction of poetic utterance is that by its intensity, its community with the very
rhythm of things and the range of its echoes in the depths
of the mind, it alone is capable of turning this *as though*
into *fact*. Such an argument would be both shortened and
strengthened if one could accept Jung's concept of the 'col-
lective unconscious' but 'entities are not to be multiplied
beyond necessity'. What I do find acceptable is that when
a poem truly fits with our experience it produces a richness
of response beyond that of ordinary language. From the
core of this response there radiate waves of emotional excitement that are rooted in our *personal* experience but at
the core of it we feel an identity with the poet. But it is not
the person we were before reading the poem who feels this
identity, for we feel ourselves enlarged by the experience.
The poet has found the words that till then had escaped
us, but now in our feeling of identity with him it is as

though we have found them ourselves. In the bringing of so rich a response, the implicit meanings which touch off echoes in the depths of our minds have an important part to play.

There is a constant struggle in non-scientific communication between 'otherness' of expression and community of perception and feeling. The poet, writing as a unique individual, feels the need for a special language and we also require him to use a special language. If he speaks the language we feel we could speak if we took the trouble, then the result is banality, e.g. Betjeman's 'Summoned by Bells.' If on the other hand he is so individual that there are too few pointers to his implicit meanings, then there are too few points of contact with our particular organisation of experience. This, I feel, is the fault of 'Altarwise by owl-light'.

What I am trying to say is made clearer by another few lines by Dylan Thomas where the individual accent is still present but where there is enough explicit meaning to touch off the response.

Now as I was young and easy under the apple boughs
About the lilting house and happy as the grass was green,
    The night above the dingle starry,
    Time let me hail and climb
    Golden in the heyday of his eyes,
And honoured among wagons I was prince of the apple towns
And once below a time I lordly had the trees and leaves
    Trail with daisies and barley
    Down the rivers of the windfall night.

On an earlier page I suggested that in *Ulysses* and *Finnegan's Wake* Joyce attempted to reproduce the quick-silver associations that quiver at all times in our waking minds. In so doing he was, we might say, making the implicit explicit. The poet also works in the depths of the mind, but

M

not in the same way. The richness of poetry comes not from making explicit what is implicit but from the fact that when thought and feeling sing together there is a stirring in the depths of the mind, an unsettlement, a tension which when it is resolved, as it will be when the poet has finished his job, brings us, as the writing of the poem brought him, to a new 'point of rest'—a *new* point of rest, for it is a characteristic of the language of poetry that while it obviously works within the framework of our own experience, it itself brings experiences of a more compelling kind than we normally find outside poetry and when we reach this new point of rest we ourselves are emotionally richer.

There was the usual grain of truth underlying Oscar Wilde's quip that one man's poetry is another man's poison. He might have gone further and said that one man's poetry one year is the same man's poison the next, for as we grow emotionally our responses change. It is a quality of that poetry which we each as individuals regard as 'the best' that it is diamond-hard against the batterings of experience. The music of *Richard II* still rings as sweetly in my ears as it ever did. *Comus*, of all that Milton wrote, has to me stood up best against the winds of familiarity; the mad scene in *King Lear* still astonishes, not by a fine excess, but by its deep organic force; the superb craftsmanship of Pope still has the power to make me wonder; Hopkins's *Spring and Fall* moves me as much now as it ever did and never ceases to make me wonder that so few words could say so much. There are so many— What about Donne? And Herbert? And lines that startling rise from the page in Wordsworth's little-known known drama *The Brothers*? and . . . Only a few weeks ago in a Sunday newspaper I read a new poem by Robert Graves, 'This Holy Month'—explicit and implicit, the statement of truth felt and perceived, set down there in print in a way that made me feel that this too was diamond-hard against 'the unimaginable touch of time'.

All non-scientific writing can be classed under the name 'the language of persuasion'. Poetry is its most concentrated form but, as Wordsworth pointed out a long time ago, science, not prose, is the opposite of poetry. What I have written in this chapter is largely true of any prose that it is not purely expository and even from the plainest of statements these elements are not entirely absent. Dryden in his *Essay on Dramatic Poesy* spoke about turning to that 'other melody' of prose. Written prose, like speech, because of its continuous nature must have a certain rhythmic pattern, a rhythm of sounds inwardly heard, a rhythm of syntactical pattern. These rhythms are intrinsic in the complicated process of linguistic communication. The writer of prose outside the realm of science has normally the job of persuading the reader to read and go on reading. The rhythm of his sentences may help or hinder him in so doing. He selects what facts he likes, what analogies he likes, out of his past experience and out of them fashions a world if he is a novelist, a new pattern of thought if he is some other kind of commentator on life, in which we at least temporarily believe. All the qualities of language which we have found in poetry come into this, the rhythms looser, the images probably less tightly packed, the time longer—but all there. His triumph will depend upon how effectively he persuades us that we are not reading words but thinking, feeling, living in a peculiarly absorbing way. For the final paradox about language is that it is self-annihilating. Of the scientist's words we should be unaware because they are overwhelmed by the significance of the facts. The poet and novelist should give us so absorbing an experience that we are unaware of the medium through which this came about. And yet they cannot achieve this without themselves exploring the possibilities and limitations of the words they use.

THE PRACTICAL ASPECT

The word 'experience' has echoed throughout this book. Words, I have said, can only be interpreted through one's own experience, but here in this chapter we have reached the position that the experience of language in poetry is itself a compelling experience. I have also discussed the relationship between words and meaning in poetry—meaning, both explicit and implicit. These ideas taken together lead to one definite conclusion about poetry in school—namely, that pupils should hear poetry as a natural part of living. They should hear it in great variety. At the early stages poems with a strong rhythm will work the greatest magic with them. There is a rich store of these in such studies of children's play as that by the Opies listed below, for the poetry read to children or read by them need not be all of the quality that brings it into the normal anthologies. The important thing is that it should not be separated out as a special subject—the poetry lesson. The separation of subjects in a time-table is always a problem. Where a school is going all out for an 'experience' programme such as described in R. F. Mackenzie's *A Question of Living* and *Escape from the Classroom* (Collins), there is no difficulty for the teacher who has a sufficient knowledge of poems to bring this or that poem in as a kind of commentary on some experience the pupils have had. But in any case even in a rigidly time-tabled school there can be few lessons so completely devoid of contact with life as to make a brief, though unhurried, reading of a poem an intrusion.

The question of meaning in poetry read to children is

much less important than the music of it. That they should listen, be interested, and yet puzzled is much more important than that they should listen, understand, and be bored.

More important still is creative work in poetry. Nearly everything I have to say on this subject is said in *The Excitement of Writing* edited by A. B. Clegg. As teachers, we habitually put completed works in front of pupils. Author, publisher, editor and printer's reader have all seen to it to the best of their ability that all the commas are in and in the right place, that there are no mis-spellings and that the grammar is as it should be. It is essential in all branches of English teaching that pupils should be made aware of the fact that nearly the whole of literature is a collection of third, fourth or fifth drafts. It is not enough to tell them this, but I am certain that a great deal about the creation of good writing can be learned even in junior classes by the communal writing of poetry, a process where creation and criticism go on side by side. In *English for the Rejected* (C.U.P.) David Holbrook comes down heavily against communal writing, but I have generally found that a class will become excited about it all as they see their poem growing before their very eyes. The essential thing is that the teacher should, to begin with, accept anything that is given in the way of a line and let the pupils make their own suggestions for improving it. Here is a poem that was composed in this way by a class reputed to be not very bright in a secondary modern school:

Our Street
Our street is grey and dark and blue
Even when the sun shines through
The gloom; and dirt of greying slates
Mingles with the drab and rotting gate.
Our street is over-run with whirling dust,

And children leave their toys to rot and rust
In huts of broken rotted wood,
And boys and girls must play in pools of mud.
At night our street is lit by gas.
I sometimes stand and watch the people pass
Beneath the rays towards the Rodney Inn
Where drunken people shout and sing.

The teacher of that class declared that apart from the general stimulus he gave by talking the only help he gave was to suggest that 'the gloom' could go in the next line. Work of this kind brings children *inside* the craft. But more than that is going on. The pupils are engaged in a sharing of experiences; they are learning from one another about finding a better way of saying what is meant; they are learning some of the rudiments of literary judgement. Creation and criticism are going on side by side and they are enjoying the experience. It seems likely that after such an experience they will look at poetry somewhat differently, one hopes as something which has to do with them and the life they live.

CONCLUSION

In this book I have dealt with some aspects of comunication that seemed to me of special importance to teachers. I am only too conscious that any one of these chapters could be expanded into a book and even that some readers may feel that there are chapters missing.

The omission of two topics in particular calls for an explanation—the teaching of reading and the teaching of grammar.

About the teaching of reading a vast amount has been written and is still being written. I have written an infinitesimal fraction of it myself and my views on the subject are given in *Reading and the Psychology of Perception* and *In Spite of the Alphabet*. The actual teaching of reading, although it is one of the most important tasks of the primary school, is a side-issue in the field of communication. Print is essentially speech made visible; communication takes place only after the print has been translated into inner or overt speech. Although I have not in this book dealt with the process of actually learning to read, most of the book is by implication concerned with reading since the process of putting meaning into words is the same whether the word is in print or in waves of sound.

Grammar? I wrote a lengthy chapter on this topic and then threw it out because I found it impossible to write about grammar in up-to-date terms without becoming involved with epistemological niceties that were out of place in this book. Some years ago I wrote a little book called *Learning and Teaching English Grammar* in which I attempted to align a fairly orthodox grammar with a theory of communication. I still think that this is what has to be done with grammar, but ideas about grammar at the moment are in a state of considerable confusion. In recent years a great deal of work has been done in this field by linguistic experts. The old Latinate grammar has been severely attacked, but a more modern grammar within the compass of even secondary school children has not yet been formulated. 'Bring us your problems and we will complicate them for you,' has been suggested as a suitable motto for a research institute. A process of complication seems to be necessary before a simplifying vocabulary can be found. The process of complicating is at present going on apace at linguistic centres and I have not yet met a linguist in full touch with current thought on this subject who claimed that what the linguistic school has to say about grammar so far is suitable for anyone below sixth form level and it may be some time before a way of presenting modern grammar is found. According to W. H. Mittins in *A Grammar of Modern English* (Methuen, 1962), 'A fully "respectable" teaching-grammar cannot be expected until a complete description of English usage is provided. Professor Randolph Quirk and a London University team are engaged upon such a description, but have years of work yet to do.' I cannot myself help feeling from present indications that we can expect nothing in this line for some time except what is far too highly specialised and formalised for school use And yet I feel that the study of grammar in the context of communication is a necessary part of a humane education.

Grammar is present whenever two words stand in a logical relationship to one another. To ask a child whether it was the dog or the kennel that was small in the sentence, 'It was a very small dog for such a big kennel', is to ask him a grammatical question, but the study of the abstract relationships between words or 'word-clusters' is hardly a primary school job. There, self-expression through words both spoken and written and the understanding of the expressions of others through listening and reading are paramount. At the secondary stage grammar is important in so far as it reveals aspects of how we think and is an arid study when not seen to be connected with the dynamics of communication.

A great deal of what I have written in this book has no *direct* application to teaching in the primary school. There is no point, for example, in telling a young child that meanings do not come across with the words. But no one should leave school for good without having reflected upon the implications of that fact. There are, however, in this book very few sentences which do not have a bearing upon the art of teaching, for a teacher is a communicator. In thinking about the nature of communication he is thinking about the grammar of his art. I hope this book will be a stimulus to creative thinking in that direction.

A BOOK LIST

WHEN I came to this part of the book, I began writing the word 'bibliography' at the top of the page and had just reached the letter 'o' when it occurred to me that, although it is itself a printed word and concerns vast quantities of print, that word has much in common with the non-linguistic symbols, the bank manager's office, the woman's hair-do, for it is sometimes the author's way of saying: 'Look at all the books I've read. You can't say I don't know what I am writing about.' So I wrote 'A Book List' instead.

In the list given below I have put books which explore various regions of the territory touched upon in this book. I have left out books that turn language into jargon. One or two of them are fairly formidable but that is only because they are long and deal with complicated matters not because they set out to impress.

A few comments on the inclusion of some books seems necessary. Ogden and Richards's almost venerable *The Meaning of Meaning* is here because it has been so influential in this field. I think it should be consulted as well as the summary in Chase's *Tyranny of Words*. I would draw special attention to Rosamund Harding's *The Anatomy of Inspiration*. It is an excellent book to start off with because it contains so much information from the *inside*; the material largely comes from the lives and letters of creative men and women in all the major branches of culture. On a much grander scale dealing largely with the same topic is Arthur Koestler's *The Act of Creation*. Civilisation would not have much to fear from its educational systems if the majority of its teachers, starting with *The Anatomy of Inspiration*, worked their way through to *The Act of*

180

Creation, putting the right meanings into the words. My final hope is that reading the very much smaller *Language for Teaching* will help the readers of it to avoid putting the wrong meanings into other people's words.

Bartlett, Sir Frederick *Thinking* (Allen and Unwin) 1958.

Chase, S. *The Tyranny of Words* (Allen and Unwin) 1935.

Clegg, A. B. (Ed.) *The Excitement of Writing* (Chatto and Windus) 1964.

Graham, A. C. *The Problem of Values* (Hutchinson) 1961.

Harding, R. *An Anatomy of Inspiration* (Heffer) 1948.

Hayakawa, S. I. *Language in Thought and Action* (Allen and Unwin) 1957.

Hoggart, R. *The Uses of Literacy* (Chatto and Windus) 1957.

Keller, Helen *The Story of My Life* (Hodder and Stoughton) (1959 ed.)

Koestler, A. *The Act of Creation* (Hutchinson) 1964.

Langer, S. K. *Feeling and Form* (Routledge) 1953.

Lewis, M. M. *How Children Learn to Speak* (Harrap) 1957.

MacMurray, J. *The Boundaries of Science* (Faber and Faber) 1939.

Ogden, C. K. and Richards I. A. *The Meaning of Meaning* (Routledge) 1924.

Russell, B. *An Outline of Philosophy* (Allen and Unwin) 1927.

Savory, T. H. *The Language of Science* (Deutsch) 1953.

Stern, C. *Children Discover Arithmetic* (Harrap) 1953.

To put books I had written myself into so distinguished a list did not seem to me fitting. The non-linguistic symbols into which they would turn in that context would not have the effect I wanted, Yet there is a good reason why four of them should be mentioned. It is that in a way they form extended prefaces to this book. Since these four books extend over a decade complete consistency need not be looked for. If I were to re-write them now, some passages would not be so simple, others would be mellower in tone, but they all have this in common with one another and with this present one: the belief that a theory of communication is basic equipment for the teacher.

Learning and Teaching English Grammar (Chatto and Windus) 1946.

Reading and the Psychology of Perception (2nd Im. Ray Palmer) 1963.

Arithmetic in the Decimal Age (Ray Palmer) 1963.

In Spite of the Alphabet (Chatto and Windus) 1965.

INDEX